Best Pucking Kiss

A Fake Relationship Hockey Romance

JULIA SAVAN

SPORTS ROMANCE AUTHOR

Developmental Editor: Erin Carter

Line Editor: Kerry Sayer

Cover Art: Moon (@illustrated.by.moon on Instagram)

Danielle and Jackie—thanks for being there through every twist and turn of this journey.

Favour—It was so much fun putting this playlist together with you. You're a real champ!

THE PLAYLIST

Automatically in Love by Carly Rae Jepsen

Thinkin' Bout Me by Morgan Wallen

Scared to Be Lonely by Martin Garrix & Dua Lipa

House Party by Sam Hunt

Slow Hands by Niall Horan

Someone You Loved by Lewis Capaldi

Watermelon Sugar by Harry Styles

Rumors by Lizzo

The Champion by Carrie Underwood

Make It Up To You by Julia Michaels

Hold On by Justin Bieber

Brother by NEEDTOBREATHE

Fight Song by Rachel Platten

Hall of Fame by The Script ft. will.i.am

The Greatest by Sia

On Top of the World by Imagine Dragons

Perfect by Ed Sheeran

Find the Best Pucking Kiss Playlist on
https://www.youtube.com/@JuliaSavanBooks

CONTENTS

CHAPTER 1

FAYE

The rich aroma of freshly baked croissants mingles with the sharp tang of espresso, enveloping me in a comforting embrace.

I artfully arrange the final touches on a tray of vibrant sandwiches.

Each one is a miniature masterpiece, a picture of Snowfield Springs' hockey team—The Snowfield Blizzards.

Their signature red and icy blue hues wink back at me.

From the tangy blue-tinted mayo to the bed of crisp micro-greens and crunchy red cabbage slaw…it's beautiful…and not my style.

I'm a baker, not a chef, for crying out loud.

But beggars can't be choosers.

Getting a call from the Snowfield Spring Blizzard's coach had totally made my morning. A breakfast order! Only, I was expecting muffins and cupcakes, not a batch order of sandwiches.

With a flourish, I spear a tiny Blizzards logo flag through each sandwich.

I can't help but wonder how Ben, my delivery boy, had managed to find them at the last minute.

I turn to survey my crew—Maria in the kitchen, and Tom at the espresso machine.

They're the reason this place hasn't folded like so many predicted when I first opened up in Snowfield Springs a few years ago.

The bell above Kiss and Crumble jingles merrily, followed by a gust of frosty Massachusetts air that sends the New Year's decorations swaying.

I can't bear to take them down yet, even though we're already a week into January.

They remind me of the night Cara convinced me to move here, just months after she landed her job at the Snowfield Medical Center.

"Come on, Faye," she'd said, her voice crackling through my tiny New York apartment. "Snowfield needs your baking magic. And I need my best friend from high school."

Two years later, here I am, still trying to grow beyond our loyal, but small, customer base.

The door finally slams shut and Officer Doug Daniels saunters in, his ample belly preceding him like a stagecoach driver.

"Morning, Faye!" His booming voice carries over the gentle clatter of dishes and the murmur of conversation. "Whoa, baby! You've outdone yourself with those beauties!"

I toss him a bright smile, never breaking the rhythm of my work.

"The usual, Officer Doug?"

He nods, eyes twinkling eagerly as he takes the maple-glazed doughnut with bacon sprinkles and a steaming cup of black coffee.

He sighs happily as he takes a bite.

"Oh, this always makes my morning! Though these doughnuts aren't helping my figure," he adds, patting his stomach with a chuckle. "How are you doing, young lady?"

"Busy, but just the way I like it."

Finally, my muscles are aching from work. Not from staring wistfully out the window for new customers.

As if on cue, Betty "Bee" Thompson glides through the door in a whirlwind of sunny yellow cashmere and clanking vintage necklaces.

"Faye, darling! Sandwiches?" Her keen gaze zeroes in on my tray, a shocked twinkle in her eye.

I hold up a sandwich, turning it to catch the light.

"Blizzards-inspired sandwiches for the boys in blue...and red!" I flash her a conspiratorial wink. "I finally got my first large order from their coach!"

Bee claps her gnarled hands in delight, her ever-present canary-hued scarf fluttering.

"Oh, they're going to flip for these! Your creativity never ceases to amaze me, sweet girl."

Basking in the warmth of her praise, I carefully slot the last sandwich into place, taking a moment to admire the colorful view.

Pride swells in my chest, only to pop like a soap bubble when I glance at the vintage cat clock on the wall.

Its swishing tail seems to mock me as realization sinks in with a sickening lurch.

Ben is late...too late. Who'll deliver these?

I blow out a harsh breath, mentally girding myself for a trek into the testosterone-fueled lion's den.

With a mental shrug, I reach for my trusty jacket, stroking its Kiss and Crumble logo.

The puffy purple monstrosity clashes magnificently with my copper-red curls—shoulder-length and wild as ever despite my attempts to tame them this morning.

I wrestle it over my flour-dusted blouse, adding an oversized stripey scarf and a slightly misshapen knit beanie to complete my winter ensemble.

Grabbing the box, I head for the door, shoulders squared for battle. "I'm heading out!" I call out to the kitchen.

Maria pokes her head out, her dark ponytail swishing behind her.

"Got it, boss!" She grins, then disappears back into her domain of rolling pins and pastry cream.

Tom waves from behind the espresso machine, steam wreathing his tattooed arms. "Good luck with the hockey boys!"

I'll need it.

Bee calls after me, her voice pitchy with mischief. "Go wow them, tiger! And see if you can wrangle some juicy gossip while you're at it."

Officer Doug dissolves into a good-natured chuckle.

Sneaking a peek back over my shoulder, I stick out my tongue. "No promises, Betty!" And with that, I whisk out the door in a jingle of bells and a swirl of icy air.

***

The snow-capped Berkshire Mountains roll by in a picturesque blur. I take the winding roads at a gentle pace, one hand on the wheel while the other guards my precious cargo of gourmet sandwiches.

If those Hallmark holiday movies were real, this would totally be the part where I get into a cutesy fender bender with a hunky lumberjack and we fall madly in love.

Unrealistic, but a girl can dream!

Humming along to the radio, I lose myself in a daydream as I pull into the bustling Snowfield Arena parking lot.

Visions of a dashing hockey player sweeping me off my skates and into a soul-searing kiss mid-ice dance through my head.

I'm a hopeless romantic with a capital H.

Blame it on an adolescence spent bingeing rom-coms and devouring grocery store bodice-rippers.

With a resolute nod, I crank up the radio, belting out an off-key rendition of "Livin' on a Prayer" as I pull into the Snowfield Arena lot.

The sprawling steel and stone structure looms like a coliseum, its soaring glass atrium winking in the winter sun.

With a confident toss of my fiery curls, I march into the arena, head held high. At twenty-two, I'm living my dream as the youngest cafe owner in town.

Making the move from New York to be closer to my best friend, Cara, still has to be the craziest decision I've ever made.

But it's not like I have anything in New York besides a mother who thrives on short marriages to old Wall Street men.

Here, I managed to set up my little slice of heaven, the Kiss & Crumble Bakery Cafe—my pride, joy, and occasional pain in the butt. But I wouldn't trade it for all the big apples.

And this is my first big order. What if they like it so much that they start ordering daily?

After what feels like a twelve-mile trek in my worn-down Chucks, I finally reach the corridor leading to the locker rooms…right as the team comes thundering down the stairs.

They're all freshly showered, smelling like a heavenly mix of cold wintergreen and testosterone.

They make quite the sight in their snug Under Armour outfits and wet gelled hair.

Wait.

I pull out my phone, rereading the text instructions from Coach Bates.

Coach Bates:

> *Leave them in the lounge as a pleasant surprise after practice.*

Shucks. Guess my dawdling daydreams made me fashionably late.

I pick up the pace, half-jogging, half-prancing down the concrete steps towards the locker room.

Just as I'm mentally congratulating myself on my Grace Kelly-esque balance, the tip of my scuffed mint-green Chuck catches on an abandoned sports bag.

The sandwiches take flight as I pitch forward.

For a slow-motion instant, a beautiful kaleidoscopic arc of red and blue fills the air like Fourth of July fireworks.

A startled "Oof!" escapes my glossed lips as I collide with a rock-solid chest.

My eyes snap up, meeting intense espresso-black eyes framed by thick dark lashes, and my heart stutters.

That scar—the jagged little lightning strike above his right eyebrow. I know this face!

It's none other than Tristan 'The Blade' Bane. The man whose posters probably grace half the teenage bedrooms in Snowfield Springs.

His burly arms link around my waist as we go pinwheeling backward until his broad shoulders thud against the painted cinder block wall.

Meanwhile, my hands have migrated from his pecs to twine around his corded neck.

Our fronts are pressed together tighter than two pages in a steamy romance novel.

And suddenly I realize two things…

One, my legs have somehow wrapped around his lean hips like a koala clinging to a eucalyptus branch, and two—*oh God*—my lips are pressed against his.

The ten-year age gap between us feels electric and dangerous. He's thirty-two, a seasoned hockey star, while I'm fresh into my twenties, running a struggling bakery.

This is so not how I planned to meet the town's most eligible bachelor.

This was so not on my to-do list.

And as for him…

Instead of pulling back and slamming me on the floor like I expected, his tongue darted across my lip. It's so fast that I almost don't notice. Slowly, he deepens the pressure, his mouth moving over mine in a soft, sensual exploration.

This time, my eyelids flutter closed as I melt into the solid heat of his body, my traitorous fingers sliding up his nape to tangle in the silken strands of his hair.

Peppermint. He tastes like peppermint and Haribo Gummies.

A low sound rumbles in his chest, half growl, half groan, and I feel the vibrations all the way to my toes.

His tongue teases the seam of my lips, one questing hand gliding down my spine to settle possessively on the small of my back.

This is wrong. This is so, so wrong. I shouldn't be kissing Tristan Bane in the concrete depths of the arena, like some tarted-up hockey bunny.

But...it's not one of those namby-pamby barely-there brushes of mouth-on-mouth.

No. This is a full-on, Molly Ringwald and Michael Schoeffling at the end of Sixteen Candles type of smooch.

The kind of earth-shaking, butterfly-inducing kiss I've been fantasizing about since my first viewing of The Notebook at age thirteen.

Only instead of Ryan Gosling in the rain, I've got Tristan Bane, and it's the best pucking kiss.

You need to step away from the man, Faye!

Before I can execute my brilliant retreat, the click-click of camera shutters shatters the charged air.

The flash of lens lights explode behind my closed lids, jarring me back to cold, cruel reality.

With a soft pop, I wrench my lips from Tristan's, eyes snapping open in dilated horror.

A horde of paparazzi surrounds us, telephoto lenses glinting as they circle like jackals around a fresh kill.

Tristan's teammates are hooting and catcalling, slapping each other on the backs like they've just witnessed the play of the century.

Mortification sears through me, setting my cheeks ablaze. Jerking back like I've been scalded, I blink down at the aftermath.

The floor is covered in an explosion of gourmet sandwiches. Anger licks through the humiliation, its bite as clean and bitter as unsweetened espresso.

Wrenching my now-shaking hands away from Tristan's traitorously muscled chest, I take a hasty step back, glaring at the epic wreckage through narrowed eyes.

"Outstanding work, Faye," I mutter, letting my hair fall forward to curtain my scorched cheeks.

"Just. Freaking. Fantastic."

Tristan just stands there smirking, cool as a cucumber in a bowl of hot sauce.

Like being caught in a liplock with a virtual stranger while knee-deep in sandwiches is a regular Tuesday for him.

"You gonna make this a habit, Red?" he drawls in a voice that's pure melted chocolate and sex, while twirling one of my crimson curls around his finger.

With what sounds like a purr, he watches it spring back upon release.

"Not that I'm complaining, but a guy likes to be wined and dined before he gets jumped."

Blood pounds in my ears as I snap my gaze to his. I'm immediately pulled in by his smoky-black eyes.

His straight, jet-black hair is slicked back, exposing a surprised smirk and eyes filled with heated attraction.

My gaze drifts upward to the signature scar above his right eyebrow and a sassy soundbite dances at the tip of my tongue.

But before I can unleash it, a metallic glint catches my eye, drawing my attention to the floor.

My name tag. It must've fallen off during our little…encounter.

Tristan, clearly unbothered by the chaos, swipes it up in one clean sweep. "What's your name, Red?"

Kissing the town's resident playboy is one thing. But staying behind for a kiss and tell? No way.

Hands trembling, I hastily turn around, feet pounding against the floor with each stride.

I'm running. I'm freaking running. Of all the romance female leads I thought I'd become someday, Cinderella just got bumped to the top of the freaking list.

CHAPTER 2

TRISTAN

The roar of the crowd slams into me like a physical force as I race down the ice, my skates carving through the rink's scarred surface.

The timer ticks down the final seconds of the third period, red digits glaring.

We are tied 3-3 with the Hawks, and I'll be damned if I let them sneak one past us now.

But with each powerful stride, a bolt of agony lances through my left knee, the muscles seizing in a vicious knot.

I grit my teeth until my jaw aches, sweat and pain stinging my eyes.

Suck it up, Bane. No one can know. Squeal about this bum leg, and you're yesterday's news.

I catch a flash of black and gold in my periphery—their center, Sanders, angling for the puck.

Putting on the speed, I lunge to intercept him...and falter as my right leg gives a sickening *pop*. "Fuck."

The puck skitters away, and the Hawk bastard pounces.

"Tristan, defense!" Doc's bellow reverberates across the ice, even as he crouches between the pipes, stick at the ready.

Oh, I'll defend, alright. If it's the last damn thing I do.

Grinding my molars, I throw myself after the center, my vision narrowing to the puck dancing on his blade. Just a little closer, one good check...

But I'm too slow, movements clumsy and sluggish with pain replacing blood in my veins.

The Hawk sidesteps me like a freaking orange cone. With a deft snap of his wrist, the puck sails over Doc's blocker...into the net.

The goal light blazes red. Foghorn blaring.

The game clock hits triple zeroes.

We lost. 4-3.

The Snowfield Springs Blizzards' first defeat of the season right before preliminaries...and it's all my fault.

***

In the locker room, the atmosphere's about as festive as a funeral. Guys slump on the benches, blank-eyed and shell-shocked.

The silence presses down like a weight, thick enough to choke on.

Diesel, our star forward, chucks his elbow pads into his locker with more force than necessary.

"What the hell was that hot mess out there, Blade? You skate like you have a crowbar shoved up—"

"Can it, Diesel," Magic Martinez cuts in, his dark eyes narrowed. "We're all pissed, but sniping at each other ain't gonna fix jack."

I look away, shame scalding my throat. Diesel is right. I let the team down, left them hanging when they needed me most.

Some freaking captain I am.

I open my mouth to…apologize? Defend myself? Crack a dumb joke to break the tension? But Coach's gravelly rumble beats me to the punch.

"Bane. My office. Now."

Well, shit.

I pull the athletic tape tighter around my knee, wobbling up on the other leg. The familiar compression brings relief, even if it's just temporary.

A few more games. I just need to hold it together for a few more.

Head down, I follow Coach's broad back through the tunnel, my uneven footsteps echoing in the close confines.

Fluorescent lights flicker overhead, painting everything a pale white. The perfect ambiance for a reaming.

I barely have one cheek on the chair before Coach lays into me. "Tristan, what on God's green earth was that shit show tonight?"

He doesn't raise his voice.

That's the worst part. He just stares at me with those faded blue eyes, his chubby cheeks frozen in a scowl. Disappointment radiates off him in waves, and it cuts deeper than any screaming tirade.

"Coach, I…" I swallow hard, the words clogging in my throat like wet cement. How can I explain without giving away my secret? Instead, I settle for, "I'm not on my A-game. It won't happen again."

His gaze drills into mine, searching. Knowing. Finally, he expels a weary sigh.

"Son, I've been around this sport longer than you've been sucking air. I know an injury when I see one."

My head jerks up, denial ready to fly. But one look at Coach's weathered face, and the fight whooshes out of me like a punctured tire. He knows.

Of course he knows.

"What I don't get," Coach continues, rubbing his fingers on the table, "is why you're so hellbent on hidin' it. This lone wolf crap is gonna bite you in the ass, kid. Let us help."

I laugh, and even I wince at the jagged bitterness coating the sound.

"Sure, Coach. I'll just waltz up to management and announce I'm damaged goods. Again. I'm sure they'll throw a freaking parade."

Last season, I wrecked my shoulder in the playoffs. Kept it hush-hush, popping Tylenol like Tic Tacs and playing through the pain.

When the higher-ups found out, they benched me faster than a drunk streaker.

I can't risk an encore. Not if I want to keep my spot on the roster. My place on the team.

Hockey is all I have, the only thing I'm good at. *Without it...I'm nothing. Nobody.*

Coach's face softens, understanding smoothing the stern lines. He opens his mouth, but I push to my feet, favoring my bad leg.

"I've got this handled. I'm seeing Dr. Emi Taylor and all."

And before he can argue, I bolt. The perfect end to a perfect fucking night.

***

I should've known the media ambush was coming.

25

The second I limp into the lobby, a barrage of camera flashes explode in my face.

Microphones jab at me from all angles. The reporters shout over each other in a cacophonous din.

"Tristan! What happened out there?"

"Are you worried your age is catching up to you?"

"How much longer can your body handle the grind of pro hockey?"

"Are you considering a buy out before the championship?"

Each question is a serrated blade to the gut, flaying me open under the harsh glare of the spotlight.

My hands clench into fists, straining against my cellphone...and the cold rectangular feel of a name tag.

Her name tag.

I want to scream, to rage, to punch something until my knuckles bleed and the voices finally shut the hell up.

But I can't afford to lose it. Not here, not now, with a zillion smartphone cameras rolling and Twitter starving for a meltdown to meme into oblivion.

So I suck a breath through my nose and hold it for a five-count.

Play it cool, Bane. Don't give the gossip buzzards more fodder. Just paste on a smirk and—

"Tristan!" A chipper female voice rises above the clamor, sugary-sweet. "What's the scoop with you and that mystery woman? The one you kissed this morning?"

I blink, my brows scrunching. *Is that what they're calling her?*

Even as the memory crystallizes—mid-length curls, pixie features, wide blue eyes blinking dazedly up at me—the reporter presses on, her grin shark-bright under the camera lights.

"Rumor has it she's your new squeeze. Can you comment? What's her name? What about your ex, Juliana?"

More voices chime in, the questions pelting me like paintball bullets.

I can't help but flinch at the name, *Juliana*. I've been around the block enough to know when I'm dating a crazy woman.

Thankfully, I was able to cut the schizophrenic figure skater off.

"Tristan! Over here!"

"Come on. The people need deets!"

"Is she just another name on your list or is she your girlfriend?"

The people need to mind their business.

I stand there, shell-shocked with each mention of Faye, my head spinning at the sudden realization. They think she's my...

I reach into my pocket again, fingers grazing the plastic edge of her name tag. *Faye.*

A jolt of electricity zaps through me at the memory of her lush curves pressed to my chest, her honey-sweet taste as our mouths melded.

In a snap, I'm somewhere else, far away from the dank arena and the circling piranhas.

A deserted beach, waves crashing against the sand. Salt and the smell of summer are carried on in the balmy breeze.

Faye's running toward me in slow-motion, fiery curls streaming behind her like a silken banner. Impossibly blue eyes sparkle with mischief and invitation.

My pulse quickens as she reaches me, sand dusting her bare toes, the strings of her tiny yellow bikini swaying with each bouncing step.

"Tristan," she gasps, my name a song on her rose-petal lips, "you're all I want. Kiss me…"

She goes up on tiptoe, arms twining around my neck, her sun-warmed skin sliding deliciously against mine.

I bend to her, like a starving man at a buffet. I feel her smile bloom against my mouth just as—

"Tristan? Yoo-hoo!" An insistent hand waves in my face, snapping me out of the daydream. "Any comments? Are you two an item or what?"

My lips still tingle with the phantom pressure of Faye's, a low ache pulsing from my lips to my groin.

Fuck, I want it to be true. I want her so bad I can hardly see straight.

But wait, aren't they supposed to be digging into my terrible play? Trying to figure out why?

For some damned reason, Faye is more than enough to distract them from my secret.

In the face of a relationship scandal of their golden Casanova, everything else is irrelevant.

Kind of disappointing. But I can't shake these vultures off entirely, not without raising red flags.

But I can throw them off the injury scent. Give them something juicier to chew on.

So I shoot the reporters a cryptic grin, my eyes heavy-lidded and hooded. "About my...excuse me. I meant, about Red...wouldn't you like to know?"

A shocked ripple goes through the crowd, their eyes bugging out. Then they go nuts, hooting and scribbling in their stupid little notebooks.

They fire off more questions, but I'm already moving, wading through the human puddle.

As I step into the crisp night air, arctic wind biting at my cheeks, I allow myself one last secret smile.

Faye's adorably awkward grin filling my mind with warmth from the inside out.

You and me, Red? This is gonna be fun...

CHAPTER 3

FAYE

Kisses are normal. I've had kisses. I'm not a blushing virgin. No biggie.

Then why! Why on earth did that minute-long kiss replay endlessly in my mind over and over again, filling me with a need that numerous showers couldn't quench?

Actually, I know why. I've never had one with a thirty-two-year-old hockey god.

I'm still in a daze as I lace up my running shoes and step out of my cozy apartment for a morning jog.

The January chill bites at my cheeks, and a fresh blanket of snow crunches under my feet with each step.

The streets of Snowfield Springs are bustling with weekend activity.

My mind is miles away, stuck replaying that electrifying moment with a certain dark-haired, blue-eyed hockey hunk.

Should I go to church for a confession? Will that cleanse my mind?

Lost in thought, I nearly plow into a cluster of teenage girls gathered on the sidewalk, their high-pitched chatter jolting me back to Earth.

"Oh my god, it's her! Blade's Red!" one of them squeals, bouncing on her toes like an overexcited Chihuahua. She's decked out in a Blizzards jersey that's more glitter than fabric.

"The Kiss & Crumble girl!" another pipes up, waving her bedazzled phone in my face. "Can we get a selfie?"

I blink, feeling like I've stumbled into an alternate universe where I'm actually not the boring girl who bakes for a living.

"Um, I think there's been a misunderstanding," I stammer, trying to edge past their designer sneakers. "I'm not—"

But Glitter Jersey is already shoving her phone under my nose, and I find myself staring at a photo that makes my cheeks flame hotter than my bakery's ovens.

It's me and Tristan, locked in a steamy embrace that definitely looks more Harlequin cover than happenstance.

The caption reads: *"Blade Scores Off the Ice: Hockey Hottie Caught Kissing Mystery Redhead!"*

Kissing and Crumbling: Valentine's Day came early.

My God, who wrote these?

I'm pretty sure my face is now the same shade as my hair.

"That's not...we're not..." I sputter, but the girls are already giggling and hash-tagging faster than I can backpedal.

Cheeks burning, I make a hasty retreat, booking it like the Wicked Witch of the West is on my tail.

Stupid, stupid, stupid! You just had to go and smooch the most notorious player in town. Way to keep a low profile, Faye!

By the time I reach the safety of my apartment, my legs are jelly and my mind is spinning fast.

I fumble for my keys, praying my housemate Cara is not yet back from her night shift at the hospital.

No such luck. As soon as I step inside, I'm greeted by a wolf whistle, a flash of hot pink scrubs, and a mess of blonde hair.

"Well, well, well," Cara says with a smirk, waggling her eyebrows at me over her steaming cup of coffee. "Looks like someone had quite the eventful delivery run yesterday."

I groan, burying my face in my hands. "You saw it too?"

"Honey, I think the only person who hasn't seen it is the Dalai Lama. And even he's probably scrolling through Twitter as we speak."

Cara gives me a sympathetic pat on the shoulder.

"Spill. How was Casanova McHockeyBuns in the lip-lock department?"

I can feel my blush deepening to fire-engine-red levels. "Cara! It was an accident!"

But even as the words leave my mouth, I can't help but replay the kiss in vivid, hormone-fueled detail.

The firm press of Tristan's muscles against my softer curves, the feel of his stubble against my skin, the way his tongue—

"Earth to Faye!" Cara snaps her fingers in front of my face, grinning like a smug cat. "You were saying?"

I shake my head, trying to dislodge the X-rated thoughts. "It didn't mean anything," I insist, more to myself than to her. "I tripped, he caught me, our lips just sort of...collided. End of story."

Cara looks like she's about to argue, but mercifully, my phone chooses that moment to ping with an incoming text.

I seize it like a lifeline, grateful for the distraction.

It's from Ben, my adorably geeky teenage delivery boy.

His message is a jumble of emojis and exclamation points, but I manage to decipher the gist: business at Kiss & Crumble is booming thanks to my accidental PR stunt.

Ben:

> *OMG, Faye, the shop is SLAMMED!*

> *Everyone wants to try Red's cakes.*

I can't help but laugh at his enthusiasm, even as a niggle of guilt worms its way into my chest.

It feels wrong to capitalize on a misunderstanding, no matter how much it might boost sales.

Me:

> That's great, Ben! But let's not encourage the rumors, okay?

> We aren't actually dating.

Ben's reply is instantaneous.

Ben:

> Wait, so you DIDN'T mean to plant one on the Blizzards' resident bad boy?

I can practically hear his teenage mind boggling at the thought.

Me:

> It was an ACCIDENT. Tristan Bane is SO not my type.

Lies, my traitorous libido whispers. *Total lies.*

Ben:

> If you say so, boss.

> BTW, your not-boyfriend just placed a huge order for custom cakes for the team's next practice.

> Want me to cancel it?

My heart does a traitorous little flutter at the thought of Tristan placing a personal order.

I can almost picture him, lounging in an expensive penthouse with that sexy smirk on his chiseled face...

I shake myself firmly. *Stop it, Faye. He's a player, remember? In more ways than one.*

Me:

> No, don't cancel. Business is business.

> But could you do me a favor?

Ben:

Anything for you, boss lady!

I take a deep, long breath.

Me:

Send me Tristan's number from the order form. We need to chat.

Fifteen nerve-wracking minutes later, I'm staring at my phone like it's a live grenade.

After triple-checking that Cara is safely in the shower, I shakily type out a message to the contact simply labeled as "T.B."

Me:

Hi Tristan, this is Faye Williams from Kiss and Crumble.

Can we talk?

It's about that kiss...

I hit send before I can chicken out, my heart thudding against my rib cage like a rogue hockey puck.

Oh god, why did I think this was a good idea?

He's probably too busy being a star player and personal orgasm handyman to rich heiresses.

So, what if I used to stalk him after watching one of his games two years ago.

Nothing crazy.

Just a slight monitoring of his new girlfriends and latest scandals.

My phone vibrates in my hand, startling a yelp out of me.

Tristan:

Hey, Faye. Mind if we video chat now?

I nearly drop my phone in shock. Video chat? With Tristan "The Blade" Bane?

Before I can talk myself out of it, I hurry into my bedroom and close the door, catching a glimpse of myself in the dresser mirror.

Oh lord, I look like I've been dragged through a hedge backward.

I hastily run my fingers through my wild red curls and swipe on some lip gloss, trying to ignore the way my hands are shaking.

Okay, Faye, you can do this. Just be cool. Casual. Totally unaffected by his smoking hotness.

I settle cross-legged on my bed, propping my phone against a stack of "Kiss This Baker" recipe books for optimal viewing angle.

With a final prayer to the hockey gods, I tap "accept" on Tristan's video call request.

Bad idea. I nearly choke on my own tongue.

The screen fills with a close-up of Tristan's face. Those piercing dark eyes and the chiseled jaw are even more heart-stopping in high definition.

He must have just showered because his damp black hair is slick against his forehead, sending droplets of water down his face.

My eyes trail after a bead of water. From his neck to his bare, muscular chest down and down.

He's bare. As in naked. As in holy hockey sticks, I can see his abs and happy trail.

"Hey there, Red," he says with a grin, his voice a lazy rumble that I feel in places I definitely shouldn't be feeling while talking to a literal stranger. "Welcome to my humble abode."

He pans the phone around, giving me a dizzying view of his sleek, ultramodern home.

Floor-to-ceiling windows, gleaming chrome appliances, a black leather couch that probably costs more than my entire apartment...

And then he's back, smirking at me through the screen like he knows exactly what his state of undress is doing to my brain functions.

"I, um," I eloquently manage, trying to keep my eyes above chest level. "I saw the headlines. About us."

Tristan chuckles, low and disorienting. "Pretty wild, huh? Who knew one little kiss could cause such a media frenzy?"

"That's actually what I wanted to talk to you about," I say, rallying my remaining scraps of dignity. "The things you said in your interview...hinting at me being your girlfriend? People are getting the wrong idea."

Tristan's grin turns sheepish, his free hand coming up to rub the back of his neck.

I studiously ignore the way the movement makes his biceps flex.

"Yeah, about that," he mutters, his tone turning unexpectedly serious. "I may have been a bit...misleading. But I had my reasons."

I frown, my hackles rising at the thought of being used as some kind of PR puppet.

Of course, men...trying to use you for all they can.

"Reasons? What reasons could possibly justify lying about our relationship status on national television?"

Tristan sighs, his eyes flickering away from the screen.

"The truth is...I'm injured, Faye. I took a bad hit last month, and it's been throwing off my game. If word gets out that I'm playing at less than a hundred percent, it could ruin my chances at the championships."

I feel a pang of sympathy despite myself. I may not know much about sports, but I can pretty much infer how much hockey means to Tristan. It's his whole life.

"I'm sorry," I console him softly, my anger deflating. "That must be really tough. But what does that have to do with me?"

Tristan meets my gaze again, his coal-dark eyes intense even through the tiny screen.

"I need a distraction. Something to keep the media focused on my personal life instead of my performance on the ice.

And what better distraction than a secret new girlfriend that isn't one of the usuals?"

Ewww. What does he mean by that?

I blink at him, my brain struggling to catch up.

"Are you saying...you want to fake date me? For publicity?"

He nods, his expression earnest.

"Just until I'm back to fighting form. We make a few public appearances, maybe leak some cutesy couple photos...nothing too invasive. And in return, your bakery gets some killer exposure. It's a win-win."

I stare at him, my mind reeling.

A fake relationship with Tristan Bane? The man who makes my pulse race and my palms sweat just by existing in my general vicinity?

Dark memories swamp me as the arrogant face of my ex, Shaun, fills my mind.

At first, he had been so kind, so attentive. Fresh out of high school, it was my first time meeting a man like that in New York.

Before I knew it, he was living in my apartment, managing my accounts, and canceling all my outings with Cara.

Once he had sucked me in, and convinced me that he knew better, it was too late.

I became a puppet like my mother.

I breathe deeply. He can't hurt me anymore. My inner voice is firm but the layer of fear belies its strength.

My breathing slows as Tristan's face replaces Shaun's. Shaun was bad but pretended to be good. Is it possible that Tristan seems bad, but is actually good?

Tristan has conveyed this whole fake relationship as a game, a facade, but I wonder if it's really only that to him.

Does he want more out of this than he's letting on?

It's a terrible idea. A recipe for disaster. There's no way I can pretend to be in love with someone who sets my hormones on fire for real.

Or can I?

CHAPTER 4

TRISTAN

I'm not the kind of guy who brings girls flowers. Hell, I'm not the kind of guy who brings girls anything except toe-curling orgasms, period.

My romantic gestures usually lean more towards "U up?" texts at two a.m. and awkward small talk over a protein shake in the morning.

But here I am, standing in front of Kiss & Crumble with a mixed bouquet that costs more than my first pair of skates, feeling like a complete fool.

I've spent the entire drive over second-guessing myself, wondering what the hell I'm doing chasing after some small-town baker like a lovesick puppy.

You need to convince her, a little voice in my head reminds me. *No one says no to Tristan Bane.*

To be fair, she didn't exactly say no to my fake relationship proposal. She said she'd think about it.

Hence, the flowers and the intentional gesture. The way to a woman's heart. At least that's what I saw on Reddit.

My plan is in motion. The totally logical, not-at-all-insane plan to fake date a pretty woman I barely know to distract from my busted knee and flagging hockey stats.

It's already hard enough hiding my limp during strategy meetings. I needed this to work.

What could possibly go wrong except the fact that just the thought of her had me harder than a brick in my pants.

Taking a deep breath, I push open the door and step inside, immediately assaulted by the scent of sugar, spice, and everything nice.

The place is packed, the chatter of happy customers nearly drowning out the tinkling bell above the door.

And there, in the midst of it all, is Faye.

She's bent over a cake, her tongue poking out of the corner of her mouth as she carefully pipes "Happy Birthday" in looping cursive.

Her wild red curls are piled on top of her head in a messy bun, a few rogue tendrils escaping to frame her face.

She's wearing a flour-dusted apron over a vintage band tee that hugs her curves, paired with wool leggings that accentuate her long, slender legs.

Focus, Bane.

I clear my throat, taking a step towards the counter. "Hey, Red. Got a minute?"

Faye's head snaps up, her cerulean eyes widening as she takes in the sight of me and my ridiculous bouquet. "Tristan! What are you doing here?"

I shrug, aiming for casual and missing by a mile. "Just thought I'd stop by, see how my favorite baker was doing. And, uh, bring you these."

I thrust the flowers towards her like they're a live grenade, feeling my face heat up under the curious stares of the café patrons.

She looks so young and cute behind the counter, flour dusting her cheeks.

Faye blinks, setting down her piping bag and wiping her hands on her apron. "Oh. Um, thanks? You really didn't have to—"

But before she can finish, I manage to trip over my own feet like a newborn giraffe, sending myself and the flowers flying towards a nearby table.

I crash into a chair, upending it and sending a plate of scones skittering across the floor.

The café goes dead silent, every eye on me as I lie there in a tangled heap, the flowers scattered around me like some kind of demented Easter basket.

I scramble to my feet, dusting off my bruised ego and trying to ignore the snickers from a table of old ladies in the corner.

"Just, uh, trying to keep you on your toes," I quip, shooting Faye a sheepish grin.

To my relief, she laughs, shaking her head as she comes around the counter to help me up.

"Falling for me already, Bane?"

She reaches for my hand, her fingers warm and slightly sticky against mine.

I feel a jolt of electricity at the contact, my skin tingling like I've just downed a triple shot of espresso.

Get it together, man. She's just a girl.

But as I let her pull me to my feet, breathing in the scent of vanilla and sunshine that clings to her like a second skin, I know that's a lie.

Faye is unlike any girl I've ever met, and the effect she has on me is as undeniable as it is terrifying.

Desperate to regain some semblance of control, I reach for the nearest tray of pastries and hold it aloft like a trophy.

"As an apology for the disruption, breakfast is on me today, folks! Courtesy of Kiss & Crumble's finest."

A cheer goes up from the assembled customers, and suddenly I'm surrounded by eager hands reaching for muffins and croissants.

I grin, basking in the attention like a cat in a sunbeam.

This is more like it.

This I can handle.

I spend the next half hour schmoozing with the café regulars, signing autographs, and posing for selfies in between bites of Faye's melt-in-your-mouth cherry Danish.

I make sure to extol the virtues of her baking to anyone who will listen, laying the groundwork for our little charade.

"Faye? Yeah, she's something special, all right. A real sweetheart. I'm a lucky guy."

"The blueberry scones? They're almost as delicious as the woman who makes them. Almost."

It's easy, playing the smitten boyfriend. Too easy.

The words flow off my tongue like honey, sweet and sticky and dangerously close to the truth.

The buzz in the cafe intensifies as more customers pour in, clamoring to try Faye's baked goods and thank their favorite hockey star.

The display case empties quickly, but the atmosphere remains electric as customers linger, sipping on steaming cups of rich coffee, spiced cider, and velvety hot chocolate.

"Hey, Tristan, is it true you and Faye are dating?" a customer asks, curiosity gleaming in her eyes.

"Yeah, we saw the pictures! That kiss looked pretty intense," another chimes in.

I glance at Faye, who's blushing furiously but manages a shy smile.

"Well, you know how the media can blow things out of proportion," I say with a wink. "But I can't deny that Faye is pretty amazing."

She snorts, tossing a dish towel at my head. "You really are the bane of my existence."

I catch the towel, twirling it between my fingers as I lean in closer, hopefully.

"Is that all I am?" I ask with a wink, tilting my head towards the handful of customers still lingering over their coffee, their eyes alight with curiosity.

Faye follows my gaze, her cheeks flushing as she realizes what I'm implying.

I can practically see the wheels turning in her head as she weighs her options, her bottom lip caught between her teeth.

Finally, she sighs, squaring her shoulders like a soldier going into battle. "Fine. You win."

She clears her throat, pitching her voice loud enough for the stragglers to hear.

"Tristan, darling. Stop talking about our relationship. You're making me shy."

The crowd's laughter changes to gasps and wolf whistles when she continues, "You don't have to tell everyone you're my boyfriend!"

No fucking way.

I step forward and wrap my arms around Faye, pulling her into a warm embrace. She stiffens for a moment, then relaxes against me.

The place erupts in cheers and applause followed by sneaky camera shots, and for a moment, I bask in the joy and chaos of it all.

This was turning out to be one hell of a day.

★★★

Later that evening, I find myself pacing the length of my living room, Faye perched awkwardly on the edge of my leather couch.

"You know, when you said we needed to talk, I figured you meant somewhere a little more...public," she remarks, her eyes darting around the cavernous space.

I chuckle, coming to a stop in front of her.

"And risk being overheard by some enterprising reporter? No thanks. Besides..." I gesture to the floor-to-ceiling windows that overlook the towering Berkshire mountains. "I thought you might appreciate the view."

She snorts, but I see her gaze linger on the vista, a hint of wonder in her eyes.

"Right. Because every girl dreams of being whisked away to a rich guy's bachelor pad."

I shrug, dropping down onto the couch beside her. "Hey, you're the one who wanted to keep things professional. This is me, being professional."

She raises an eyebrow, scooting pointedly away from me. "By inviting me to your home? Alone? At night?"

I hold up my hands in a gesture of innocence. "Hey, I'm just trying to make sure we're on the same page here. We need to get our story straight if we're going to pull this off."

She sighs, pinching the bridge of her nose. "Fine. Let's hear it, then. What's our cover story?"

I lean back against the cushions, propping my feet up on the coffee table.

"Simple. We met at the café, struck up a conversation, and realized we had undeniable chemistry. We've been dating in secret for a few weeks, but decided to go public after the tabloids caught wind of our little love smooch."

She gapes at me, her eyes wide. "Love smooch? Seriously?"

I grin, enjoying the flush that creeps up her neck. "It's called branding, babe. Got to give the people something to talk about."

She scowls, crossing her arms over her chest. "Don't call me babe. And what about your injury? How do we explain that?"

I wave a hand dismissively.

"They won't know. But if they do, we'll say I took a bad hit during practice, but it's nothing serious. I'll be back on the ice in no time, thanks to the tender loving care of my devoted girlfriend."

She makes a gagging noise, but I can see the hint of a smile tugging at the corner of her mouth.

"You're laying it on a bit thick, don't you think? And how is your knee, really?"

I adjust my position on the couch, unconsciously stretching out my leg. "Grade one ACL sprain. Doc says I got lucky—no tear, nothing that needs surgery. Just some PT and rest."

I run a hand through my hair, my frustration evident. "Been doing sessions with the team doctor, Emi, three times a week. That woman is a sadist with those resistance bands, I swear."

"And nobody else knows?" She leans forward, genuine concern in her eyes.

"Just Coach Thompson. He's keeping it quiet, letting me 'recover from the flu' officially." I give her a wry smile. "Can't have the vultures circling before playoffs, you know? The team doc says another few weeks of PT and I should be back in fighting shape."

Her face crumples like a piece of paper. "Does it hurt?"

"Only my pride, Red."

At her skeptical look, I add, "And maybe a little when I forget and try to walk too fast. But hey, at least I've got my own personal cover story now."

"Also, you need to be more low-key," she says, changing the subject. "That stuff today at the bakery was overboard. And I kind of... hate flowers."

Reddit lied.

"About that, I'm sorry." I sigh, leaning back. "Just giving the people what they want. And right now, they want a fairy tale romance between the town sweetheart baker and the big, bad hockey player."

She huffs, blowing a stray curl out of her face.

"This isn't a fairy tale, Tristan. It's a business arrangement. And if we're going to make it work, we need to set some ground rules."

I raise an eyebrow, intrigued despite myself. "Ground rules, huh? Do tell."

She starts ticking off points on her fingers. "First of all, no more surprise visits. We need to coordinate our schedules to maximize the PR impact."

I nod, conceding the point. "Fair enough. What else?"

She hesitates, her eyes darting away from mine. "Secondly...no more physical contact. At least, not when we're alone."

I frown, pushing off the couch to move closer to her. "What do you mean?"

She crosses her arms over her chest, a defensive gesture that sends a pang of something uncomfortably close to hurt through my chest.

"Just what I said. We keep things strictly professional when there's no one around to see. No hugging, no hand-holding, and definitely no…"

"Kissing?" I finish for her, my voice rough.

She nods, her cheeks flushing even darker. "Right. None of that."

I study her for a long moment, trying to read the emotions swirling in those sea-blue eyes. *Is that fear I see there? Disgust? Or something else entirely?*

"Okay," I say finally, scooting back. "If that's what you want, I can keep my hands to myself. But I hope you know, Red…" I let my gaze travel over her slowly, from the tips of her scuffed sneakers to the top of her fiery head. "…it's going to be a hell of a challenge."

Her breath hitches, her lips parting slightly as she stares up at me.

She yanks back like she's been burned, her eyes widening.

I frown, studying her carefully. She's so young, so fresh-faced with innocence that it makes my chest ache.

When I was her age, I was already five years into my hockey career, jaded by fame and fortune. Her doll eyes are like a balm to my cynical soul.

"You know, for someone who agreed to be my fake girlfriend, you seem awfully jumpy around me."

She flushes, tucking a stray curl behind her ear. "I'm not jumpy. I'm just...cautious. This is all new to me, okay?"

I lean in closer, my eyes locked on hers. "New to you? Come on, Red. Don't tell me you've never been in a relationship before."

She swallows hard, her gaze dropping to my mouth. "Not one like this," she whispers, her voice husky.

I feel my body tighten in response, my heart hammering against my rib cage.

I know I should back off, should respect the boundaries she's set. But God help me, I can't seem to make myself move.

"Faye," I murmur, my hand coming up to cup her cheek. "If this is too much for you, just say the word. We can call the whole thing off right now."

She shakes her head, her eyes fluttering closed as she leans into my touch. "No. I can do this. I just..."

I nod, my thumb stroking lightly over her cheekbone. Even in her lack of words, I can hear the hurt. *Who broke you?*

"Of course. We'll take things slow, go at your pace. But Faye..."

I wait until she opens her eyes, until those ocean blue depths are locked on mine. "I'm going to need you to trust me. Can you do that?"

She hesitates, her gaze searching mine for a long moment. Then, slowly, she nods.

"Okay," she whispers, her breath ghosting over my lips. "I'll trust you, Tristan."

I smile, my hand sliding into her hair to cup the back of her neck. "Good. Then kiss me."

CHAPTER 5

FAYE

One minute, I'm staring at Tristan's stupidly perfect face, my brain short-circuiting with the realization that, *holy shit, I'm actually going to kiss him.*

The next, my lips are on his, and I'm pretty sure I'm dying. Or dreaming. Or both.

It's like every romance novel cliché come to life—the world stops spinning, time stands still, and all that jazz. But damn if it doesn't feel good.

His mouth is firm and insistent, his tongue tracing the seam of my lips like he's mapping every curve and contour.

I feel like I'm being consumed, devoured, set ablaze from the inside out.

I didn't think anything could top our accidental first kiss, but this? This is next level.

This is the kind of kiss that makes you weak in the knees and stupid in the head. The kind of kiss that ruins you for all other kisses.

I'm vaguely aware of my hands fisting in his shirt, my body arching into his like I'm trying to crawl inside his skin.

He tastes like mint and lust and something unidentifiable, dark and arresting and distinctly Tristan Bane.

If ever a flavor could be described as hot sex on wheels, it would be this—all hot motors and twisted steel, fast and dangerous and impossible to ignore.

Seriously, what is it about this man that turns me into a blushing, blithering idiot? It's just a kiss, for fuck's sake. It doesn't mean anything.

Except that's a lie, and we both know it. Because when Tristan kisses me, it feels like the realest thing I've ever known.

Like my entire life has been leading up to this moment, this startling collision of lips and teeth and tongues.

Like I was made to fit against him, all curves to his hard lines, soft to his rough.

And I never, ever want it to end.

But of course, it does. He pulls back far too soon, his breath mingling with mine in the scant space between our mouths.

His eyes are hooded, his gaze dark and inscrutable as he stares down at me.

"Not bad, Red," he murmurs, his voice a low rumble that vibrates through me like a tuning fork. "Looks like we'll have plenty to work with when this show hits the road."

Why didn't I pull away?

And just like that, the spell is broken. Reality comes crashing back in, cold and unforgiving as a bucket of ice water to the face.

Right. The cameras. The ruse. The big, fat lie we're trying to sell to the world.

I slide back, my hands falling from his chest like they've been scalded. My face feels hot, my skin too tight, my breathing ragged and uneven.

Get it together, Faye, I scold myself. *Don't let him see how much he affects you.*

"Well, that was…something," I hear myself say, my voice too bright, too brittle. "Glad to see you're taking this whole thing seriously."

He grins, the twist of his lips somehow both infuriating and knee-meltingly sexy.

"Oh, I'm taking it very seriously, Red. In fact, I have a proposition for you."

I raise an eyebrow, trying to ignore the way my traitorous stomach flips at his words.

"A proposition? Why do I feel like I'm going to regret asking what that entails?"

He chuckles, his eyes glinting in a way that can only mean trouble.

"Here's the deal, we kick this charade up a notch. Make it a little more...convincing."

I frown, suddenly wary. "What do you mean, 'more convincing'? I thought we were selling it pretty well already."

He shrugs, his broad shoulders rolling beneath his sinfully tight shirt. "Sure, for the small-town gossip mill. But if we really want to throw the media off my trail, we need to go bigger. Bolder."

I stare at him, a sneaking suspicion taking root in my gut. "Tristan Bane, if the next words out of your mouth are 'sex tape,' I swear to god—"

He laughs, loud and unbridled, his head thrown back in genuine amusement.

"Jesus, Red, what kind of guy do you take me for?"

73

He sobers, his eyes finding mine, dark and intense. "I was going to say you should move in with me."

I blink. Once. Twice. Three times. "I'm sorry, what?"

"You heard me. We make like a pair of lovesick lovebirds and shack up together. Play house for a little while. Really sell the whole 'secret romance' angle."

I gape at him, my brain struggling to process the sheer audacity of his suggestion.

"Are you insane? I can't just…move in with you! We barely know each other!"

He grins, undeterred by my spluttering indignation.

"That's the beauty of it, Red. The media will eat it up—the whirlwind romance, the passion that couldn't be denied. It's gold."

I shake my head, wondering if I've somehow stumbled into an alternate universe where logic and reason no longer apply.

"No. Absolutely not. There is no way I'm going to play house with you, Tristan. It's too much."

His grin fades, his brow furrowing in confusion.

"Why not? It's the perfect plan. We can keep up appearances without constantly having to sneak around. It'll make everything so much easier."

I let out a humorless laugh, dragging a hand through my unruly curls.

"Easier for who, exactly? Because from where I'm standing, this sounds like a grand plan for trouble."

He takes a step towards me, his expression uncharacteristically serious.

"Faye, come on. Think about it—the publicity, the buzz—it could be huge for your bakery. Don't you want that?"

I hesitate, hating myself for even thinking it.

He's right, of course—living with Tristan, even just for show, would take this whole ruse to the next level.

Kiss & Crumble would be the talk of the town—hell, the whole state. The hype alone would be enough to keep me in the black for months.

But at what cost? My sanity? My self-respect? My stupid, traitorous heart?

"I don't know, Tristan," I say slowly, my resolve wavering. "It's a lot to ask. I have a life, you know. A job. Responsibilities."

"And you can still have all that," he insists, his eyes boring into mine. "Nothing has to change, not really. You'll just be…staying with me for a little while. That's all."

I bite my lip, my mind racing with the implications.

It's a bad idea. It's a colossally terrible idea, but god help me, I want to say yes.

I take a deep breath, feeling like I'm standing on the edge of a cliff, toes curled over the precipice.

"If I do this," I mutter slowly, deliberately, "we have to have rules. Boundaries. This is strictly a business arrangement, got it? No funny business."

He grins, his eyes lighting up with mirth.

"Scout's honor, Red. I'll be a perfect gentleman." He pauses, his grin turning wicked. "Unless you ask me not to."

I roll my eyes, my heartbeat slowly returning to normal. "Keep dreaming, Bane. I'm not that easy."

He winks, his laugh low and rumbling.

"Never thought you were, Red. Never thought you were. Now, I need a video of us together."

"Doing what?"

"Nothing much, just a repeat of five minutes ago."

★★★

The video hit social media within hours under a fake Instagram account.

By the next morning, my phone started blowing up with notifications from gossip blogs speculating about the "Mystery Redhead" who'd tamed small town hockey's most notorious bachelor.

I groan, sinking lower in my chair as Ben gleefully reads me the headlines between customers at Kiss and Crumble.

"Ooh, here's a good one—'Blade Scores Off the Ice: Hockey Hottie's Sweet Kiss with Local Baker.' They're calling you his 'Cinnamon Spice.' Get it? Because you're a baker and the color of your hair?"

"Ben, I will knead you into a cinnamon spiced roll in five seconds if you don't shut up now."

"Got it, boss."

***

And so, with the feeling of impending doom hanging over me like a cartoon anvil, I find myself at Tristan's ridiculous mansion one week later.

You can do this, Faye. It's just a few weeks. A couple of months, tops. You've survived worse.

But have I? Have I really? Because as the door swings open to reveal Tristan's smirking face, I'm not so sure.

He looks devastating in dark wash jeans and a white henley, the fabric straining across his broad chest in a way that makes my mouth go dry.

"Red!" he greets me, his eyes raking over my duffel bag and slightly disheveled appearance. "I was starting to think you'd changed your mind."

He laughs, low and warm, and despite myself, I feel at ease.

This is familiar territory—the banter, the back-and-forth, the simmering tension that never quite boils over.

I can do this. I can totally, absolutely, one hundred percent do this.

"So, where's my room? Preferably one with a lock on the door and a minimum of fifty feet between us at all times."

Tristan grins, snagging my bag from my shoulder and heading for the stairs.

"Right this way, princess. I put you in the east wing, far away from my nefarious clutches."

I roll my eyes, trailing after him. "How magnanimous of you. Truly, chivalry lives on."

We reach the top of the stairs, and Tristan pauses outside a black door. "Here we are," he says, his hand on the knob. "Brace yourself, Red. This might be a bit of a shock."

I frown, suddenly wary. "What do you mean, a shock? What did you—"

But my words die in my throat as he swings the door open, revealing what can only be described as a Pepto-Bismol nightmare.

Every surface, every fabric, every conceivable inch of space is awash in varying shades of pink.

"What...the...heck." I gasp, blinking rapidly in a futile attempt to clear my vision. "Did a unicorn throw up in here? Am I being hazed?"

Tristan chuckles, tossing my bag on the aggressively ruffled bedspread.

"I may have gone a touch overboard with the whole 'girl' thing. But in my defense, the lady at the store said pink was very in this season."

I turn to him slowly, my eyes narrowing to suspicious slits. "Wait a minute. Are you telling me you...decorated this room? Yourself?"

He shrugs, looking suddenly fascinated by his shoes. "I might have picked out a few things. You know, to make it more homey."

Pink doesn't equal homey, buddy.

I stare at him, dumbfounded.

"That's...strangely sweet of you," I relent slowly, a reluctant smile tugging at my lips. "In a completely misguided and vaguely insulting way."

He grins, looking inordinately pleased with himself.

"I aim to please, Red. Now, I'll leave you to settle in—dinner's at seven sharp. Wear something nice." He pauses, his eyes glinting with mischief. "Or don't wear anything at all. I'm not picky."

And with a wink and a smirk, he's gone, leaving me alone in my Pepto-tastic prison.

What have I gotten myself into?

I close my eyes, willing my pulse to slow. Surely, I can keep my head down and my heart firmly in check, no matter how tempting it might be to let myself feel something real, something true.

Because in the end, that's all this is—a feeling. A fleeting, fickle thing, as insubstantial as smoke and just as likely to slip through my fingers if I try to hold on too tight.

And I'll be damned if I let myself get burned by the likes of Tristan "love 'em and leave 'em" Bane.

CHAPTER 6

TRISTAN

I watch Faye take her first bite of my trademark carbonara.

My heart does this weird little tap dance in my chest. I've cooked for women before; it's a tried and true panty-dropper move.

But this feels different. It feels important. It feels like it matters what she thinks beyond just getting her naked and sweaty.

Bane, get a hold of it, man. Since when do you care about cooking for some chick?

But even as I am thinking it, I know the answer. Since Faye. Since this blue-eyed, fire-haired spitfire waltzed into my life and turned it upside down with a single kiss.

She chews thoughtfully, her pink lips pursing as she concentrates.

My gaze drifts to her mouth, remembering the feel of kissing her—soft and sweet and so damn addictive.

"Okay, I'll bite," she says finally, setting down her fork. "Where did you learn to cook like this? This is really good."

I shrug, ridiculously pleased by her praise. "Picked it up when I was younger. Charity spots and soup kitchens never had enough to fill me up."

Her brow furrows and a little crease appears between her eyes. "And your parents?"

I turn away, suddenly interested in the grain of the hardwood table. "Deadbeat dad. Mom put me in foster care."

I can feel her eyes on me, curious and judging. I bite my lip hard to suppress myself from squirming in the intense dislike of being this vulnerable, even over this small chip of my history.

"That must have been tough." Her tone is laced with sympathy. "I understand how hard it is growing up so well on all alone. My mother—"

Oh, no.

"Don't do that, Red."

She stops mid-chew. "Do what?"

I sigh, twirling my fork through the creamy goodness on my plate.

"Do the whole trauma magnet thing. You don't have to find a matching sock pair to my shitty childhood."

"Excuse you!" she exclaims, forearms thumping against the table's glassy surface. "If you must know, I grew up alone most of the time. My father passed away when I was a child and my mother was too preoccupied with being a perfect trophy wife to find time for me."

"Woah." I reach for a glass of orange juice, swallowing my mortification and empathy in one big gulp.

"Yes, woah…but how did you do it?"

I shrug, tension draining from my shoulders. "I pulled through with the help of some good people. One put me into junior hockey. Others kept me out of trouble, got me a scholarship to college."

I chance a glance at her, bracing myself for the pity in her eyes.

There isn't any of that, though. Just quiet understanding that makes my chest ache in a pleasant way.

"I was probably still watching Saturday morning cartoons when you were starting your professional career," she muses, twisting a strand of that glorious red hair around her finger. "Hockey more or less saved you, huh?"

I freeze, the fork halfway to my mouth.

The decade between us suddenly feels vast, but when she smiles, it shrinks to nothing.

"It did. It really did," I reply with a grin.

***

"You have to tell the truth."

I glare at Dr. Emi Taylor, my jaw clenched so tightly I'm surprised my teeth aren't cracking. "I don't know what you're talking about."

Dr. Emi Taylor just finished my ice bath therapy for the day. Her office was a mix of a clinic and physical therapy space.

Having the team's dedicated physician handle any health issues meant consistent care, even if her methods felt like torture sometimes.

The harsh lights flickered against her curly Afro, casting shadows over her white team doctor coat.

After a few minutes of intense glaring, she sighs, narrowing her dark eyes behind wire-rimmed glasses.

"The tape job should hold for practice but don't play stupid, Tristan. It doesn't suit you."

She looks over to Coach, who is looming in the middle of the room like a statue of gloom in his faded Blizzards tee. "Right, Coach?"

"I agree." Coach crosses his arms and shoots a warning glare at me.

I shift on the exam table, the rustle of the paper protesting beneath my butt. I hate these fucking checkups. The poking and prodding, the serious looks of interest, the warnings to take better care of myself.

"I'm managing," I grit out, my hands fisting at my sides. "I don't need a fucking shrink poking around in my head like a medical mother confessor of some sorts."

"I'm not a shrink or a confessor," Emi says patiently like she's explaining to a particularly dim-witted child. I can't help looking down at the floor as she goes on.

"I'm your doctor. And as your doctor, it's my job to make sure you're healthy. Both physically and mentally. You can't keep hiding from your team."

I narrow my eyes at her, hating how she can see right through me. "I'm fine. It's just a little pain."

"It's a grade one ACL tear," she groans, tapping her pen against my chart. "And it might actually get better with therapy. But if it gets worse during play, you'll need surgery. Why on earth is your pain threshold so high, Tristan?"

You don't want to know.

My stomach drops at her words, and I'm suddenly drenched in cold sweat.

It's much worse than I thought.

"How long?" I ask, my voice breaking from my throat in a hoarse rasp. "Assuming it gets worse and I need to get surgery, how long before I can play again?"

"Assuming it gets worse. Heavy on the assuming." Emi's expression turns grim, her mouth setting in a thin line.

"How long, Emi?"

"You're looking at six to eight months with surgery and proper rehab."

The world falls off its axis, the ground gives away under my feet. *Six to eight months. A whole season.*

"No," I exclaim, my voice rising to a panic. "No fucking way. I can't miss that much time. I'll be really careful!"

"Tristan," Emi grunts, her voice softening with something that sounds far too much like pity. "I know this is hard to hear. But if you don't totally get off the knee and keep playing on it, you could be looking at permanent damage. The kind that ends careers."

There must be some other way.

"Also, you need to tell the team. When I told them you were absent because of a stomachache, they didn't believe it. Everyone knows you're not one to miss practice." Coach Bates sighs.

I groan. Deep down, I know they are right.

We have competition games in a few weeks, and I'm scared of performing poorly on the rink in front of everyone.

Yet, I'm not ready to spill everything to the team.

I want to keep playing. I don't want to let the team down in the upcoming season.

The spring season and championships are only a month away. I just need more time on the ice before I can take a break and focus on getting treated.

I'm positive I can hold out till then.

Coach Bate's expression darkens.

"Tristan, I'm not saying this because I want to stop you from playing. You're one of my best players, but I need you to get proper treatment. How long do you think your fake relationship will keep the media distracted from finding out what's really going on with you?"

Oh, my God.

I almost snap my neck as I jerk around to look at Coach Bates.

"My fake relationship?" I ask, and he nods.

Three weeks of living together has settled into an unexpectedly sweet routine for me and Faye.

Everything fits together perfectly with her in my place—what I'm starting to think of as our place.

We attended press conferences where we played our parts perfectly, charity events where my hand never left hers, casual dinners at local hotspots where paparazzi 'happened' to catch us sharing dessert.

Each public performance brought knowing winks from the team, while private moments have been increasingly charged with something that feels dangerously real.

The lines between pretense and truth are blurring, and I'm not sure I want to redraw them.

"Despite your little acts for the public, I caught on to it immediately. The baker isn't really your girlfriend, is she?" Coach asks, and I stare at him quietly.

Dr. Taylor doesn't seem surprised at the reveal, so I know she's already aware.

"I actually li—"

Like her.

"Hey Cap, how's your stomachache?" Slick interrupts, sticking his head into the room. He quickly shoves his phone in his pocket as he walks over.

Diesel and Doc also come in, flanking him.

"The guys and I decided to stop by on your way home."

Guilt slices through me. "Uh…my stomach is much better. Dr. Taylor gave me some really good painkillers."

Fucking liar.

That's all I am now. I have to set this right. But at the same time, I have to find a way to continue playing, a way to stay on this team.

If that requires lying through my teeth, then fine, so be it.

***

I surface from the depths of my heated indoor pool, my lungs burning and vision blurry. The water is warm against my skin, the chlorine stinging my eyes and nose.

I don't know how long I've been down here, holding my breath until my chest aches and my head pounds.

It's a thing I do sometimes, when the pressure gets to be too much.

When I need to escape, to feel something other than the constant, gnawing fear that everything I've worked for is about to come crashing down around me.

I float on my back, staring up at the glass ceiling of my indoor pool room.

It's a ridiculous luxury. The kind of thing that screams, "I have more money than sense." But I love it, this little oasis of calm in the midst of my chaotic life.

Floating on my back is my favorite. I swim to the other edge and hit a button, switching off the pool lights.

The moon is three-quarters full and, on this clear night, the stars look down upon me through the glass ceiling with a pale blue light.

As my body drifts, so does my mind. Some would consider me lucky, and I am; I'd never deny it, but I've worked hard for everything I have.

My life wasn't always so grand. Memories flow vividly through my head.

My mother crying about having to work, cook, and feed a child. Me soon after, lost and confused as a six-year-old in the cold grasp of the foster system.

"Stop thinking about that," I groan, plunging my head underneath the surface again.

My eyes flutter closed, and I let the gentle lapping of the water lull me into a trance.

I'm so lost in the swirling vortex of my thoughts, that I don't hear the soft padding of feet on the tile.

It's not until I feel the displacement of the water, the ripples lapping against my skin, that I realize I'm not alone.

My eyes snap open, my body jackknifing into a sitting position, covered by the loud movements on the other side.

And there, stepping into the pool, is Faye.

I thought she was sleeping.

She's wearing a simple black two-piece, the kind that's more functional than fashionable. But fuck me, she makes it look like something straight off the pages of Sports Illustrated.

Her red hair is piled on top of her head in a messy bun, a few loose curls bouncing as she moves.

Her skin is pale and luminous in the moonlight. The smattering of freckles across her nose and cheeks stand out like constellations.

She hasn't seen me yet, too focused on wading into the water. I watch her, my breath caught in my throat as she slides in, her movements graceful and fluid.

Damn, she's beautiful.

The thought hits me like a punch to the gut, stealing the air from my lungs.

I've known Faye was gorgeous from the moment I first laid eyes on her, but this...this is different.

This is a visceral awareness, a bone-deep certainty that I've never felt before.

I must have made some kind of noise, because suddenly she turns, eyes widening as she catches sight of me.

"Tristan!" she gasps, her hand flying to her chest. "What the fuck—"

I grin at her, trying to ignore the way my heart is pounding. "Evening, Red. Fancy meeting you here."

She scowls at me, but there's no real heat behind it.

"You nearly gave me a heart attack. What are you doing lurking in the moonlight like some kind of creeper?"

I shrug, leaning back against the edge of the pool. "Couldn't sleep. Thought I'd come down for a swim."

She eyes me warily, like she's not quite sure what to make of me as she paddles over. "In the middle of the night?"

"Best time for it," I say easily, flashing her my most charming smile. "No distractions, no interruptions. Just me and the water."

She nods slowly, a little furrow appearing between her brows. "I get that. Sometimes it's nice to just...escape for a bit."

There's something in her voice, a wistfulness that tugs at my battered heartstrings.

I wonder what she's escaping from, what demons chase her in the quiet moments.

None of that seems to matter with her next to me, wet skin against mine.

Moonlight spills through the glass ceiling as we tread water in the center of the pool, faces turned upward to the star-scattered sky.

The water laps gently around us, our legs brushing occasionally as we float.

"Can I ask you something?" Faye says suddenly, her voice soft and hesitant.

I glance down at her, my brow furrowing. "Shoot."

She bites her lip, looking uncharacteristically nervous.

"I know it saved you, but why hockey? I mean, what is it about the game that makes you love it so much?"

I blink at her, taken aback by the question.

It's not something I've ever really tried to put into words before, the bone-deep passion I feel for the sport that's defined my entire life.

"It's..." I start, trailing off as I search for the right words. "It's the only thing that's ever made sense to me. The only thing I've ever been good at. The one place I know I won't be discarded."

Abandoned.

I take a deep breath, feeling the familiar tightness in my chest.

"When I'm on the ice, everything else just...falls away. It's like the whole world narrows down to just me and the puck and the goal. Nothing else matters."

Not my loneliness, not my lack of family, not the pain of my childhood. I'm just Blade.

I give a rueful little laugh, shaking my head as I swim back to the edge. "I know that sounds fucking cheesy, but it's the truth. Hockey is...it's everything to me."

Faye nods slowly, swimming up to join me. "I get that. It's like...like it's a part of you. Like you can't imagine your life without it."

I stare at her, feeling like she's just reached inside my chest and pulled out my still-beating heart.

How does she do that? How does she see me so clearly, so completely?

"Yeah," I say hoarsely, my voice rough with emotion. "Yeah, that's...that's exactly it."

She gives me a small, understanding smile, her blue eyes soft in the dim light.

"I feel the same way about baking. About my cafe. It's not just a job, you know? It's a part of who I am."

"And it's beautiful."

Our conversation lulls and silence reigns.

Faye's fingers reach out slowly to trace a jagged scar on my forearm, pale silver in the starlight. I can feel her unspoken question in the gentle touch.

"It's a hockey injury. Foster league game when I was fourteen." The words come easier in the dark, with only moonlight between us. "Snapped it clean when pushing a shot."

"Must have hurt like hell," she murmurs, her breath warm against my wet skin as she leans closer to assess it.

A bitter laugh escapes me and I pull away.

"The break wasn't the worst part. My foster mom at the time…" I trail off, remembering the sickly-sweet smell of chamomile compresses and the burn of tiger balm. "Let's just say she had unconventional ideas about medicine. Six weeks of herbal remedies and meditation while it healed painfully."

Faye's sharp intake of breath echoes off the glass ceiling. "Tristan…"

"I learned real quick how to push through pain after that." I force a shrug, trying to lighten the moment. "On the bright side, it gave me one hell of a pain threshold for hockey."

But Faye's eyes, shiny in the moonlight, see right through my attempted deflection.

She doesn't push though. She just twines her fingers with mine under the water. Understanding without pity. "Was she the one who introduced you to hockey in the first place?"

I shake my head, nostalgia blooming in my chest.

"No. His name was Bob…he fostered me when I was twelve. That man took in the most broken foster kid he'd ever seen."

"So he was your main influence?" Faye turns around, elbow to the tiled edge and palm to her chin as we bob slightly.

The words come easier in the dark. "Yes. He worked security at the Snowfields Hockey Arena back then."

"What was he like?"

"Everything I needed. Gruff on the outside, but…"

I swallow hard, remembering his wrinkled face crinkling with pride the first time I landed a perfect shot.

"He saw something in me worth saving. He snuck me into games after his shifts, taught me to skate on the empty rink at midnight."

"He sounds wonderful," she whispers, moving closer until I can count the freckles dusting her nose.

"He was. Saved every penny to buy me my first real skates. Said they were magic—would take me anywhere I wanted to go." My voice catches. "Sadly, he passed away before he could see me make it."

Faye's free hand comes up to cup my cheek, her thumb brushing away tears I didn't realize were there.

"He saw, Tristan. He definitely saw you. He's still watching you."

The understanding in her eyes unravels me.

I surge forward like a broken rope, capturing her lips with mine. She tastes like chlorine and moonlight and something uniquely Faye that makes my head spin.

Her arms wind around my neck as I press her against the pool wall, the water lapping gently around us.

The sounds she makes echo off the glass ceiling, mingling with the gentle splash of water, as I worship her with everything I have.

My hands find her waist, her skin cool and smooth under my palms. I tug her closer, lifting her just enough that her legs wrap around me.

She gasps into my mouth, a sound that goes straight to my brain, turning every coherent thought into static.

When I pull back to catch my breath, her face is flushed, her curls damp and clinging to her shoulders.

"Are we really doing this?" she asks, her voice a little breathless, a little shaky.

"Do you want to?" I counter, letting my thumbs draw lazy circles on her hips.

Her answer comes in the form of a kiss, more desperate this time, and it's all the permission I need.

I bring her to the shallow end of the pool and lift her onto the ledge, the water streaming off her.

My hands are everywhere—exploring, teasing, learning every inch of her like I'm studying for the most important test of my life.

I trail kisses down her neck, her collarbone, the curve of her shoulder.

Kissing around the edge of her swimsuit top, my tongue brushes over her hardened nipple.

She gasps my name as her fingers wind their way into my hair.

I go lower. Lower. And lower.

Right until my lips pause above the tight waistband of her black bottoms. My throat goes dry and my mouth moistens. *I need a taste.*

Time seems to stand still and I glance up, meeting Faye's gorgeous blue eyes with enlarged pupils.

"Can I taste you, Red?"

Her body goes rigid with a sharp intake of breath. "What did you say?"

"You heard me the first time."

A deep flush covers her chest and she tears her gaze up to the glass ceiling. "Go ahead."

Permission granted, I lay her back and peel off her swim bottoms with a quick shimmy of her hips, baring the trim mound between her pale legs.

Even in the moonlight, the red triangle of hair is bright against the puffiness of her pussy lips.

I bend down to lick the shy beaded bud with the flat of my tongue.

Faye mewls, her nails digging into my hair as she pulls me closer.

Sucking and nipping, I lean in, working her mercilessly, delighting in every breathy gasp and wanton writhe of her body.

I reach my hands upward, my fingers trace teasing trails up her ribs and down her quivering belly, as I switch my attention to her other breast.

"Tristan." My name is a broken plea on her lips as my tongue clears a gentle path through her soaked folds. "Oh God, please…"

Slowly, carefully, I ease my tongue inside her, reveling in the vise-grip of her walls.

Her soft ass jumps off the tiled edge, almost dunking me back into the pool.

"Easy, Red."

"I'm trying. It's just...I can't control it."

Despite her whimpers and complaints, I come back to the pool's edge, bringing my lips again to the throbbing petals around her clit.

A finger slides into her, followed by another, pumping in time to the hungry pull of my other hand on her nipple.

Faye bucks in my face with abandon, her inner muscles fluttering like hummingbird wings as I bring her closer and closer to ecstasy.

"That's it," I tell her, sucking noisily on her swollen clit. "Just let go."

With a high, keening wail, she shatters, her release pulsing hot and wet around my lips.

I work her through it with tender strokes, gentling her down from the peak.

I gently gather Faye in my arms, her face buried in the sweat-slick hollow of my throat.

"You," she murmurs dreamily, pressing a clumsy kiss to my thundering pulse, "are really good at that."

I chuckle lowly, cradling her close as post-orgasmic tremors wrack her frame. "You haven't seen nothin' yet, Red. I'm just getting started with you."

CHAPTER 7

FAYE

The glow of the TV illuminates Tristan's chiseled features as he lies beside me on the plush couch, one muscular arm draped lazily over my shoulders.

My limbs feel like lead. But in a good way. It's the type of feeling that comes from a heavy combination of hot hockey god and skillful fingers.

The pool drained me in more ways than one.

Tristan had to carry me out of the pool to the shower to get all the chlorine off.

I didn't have to lift a finger, down to the moment he pulled his t-shirt over my head.

On screen, the sassy ladies of Two Broke Girls banter and scheme, their Brooklyn accents filling the air.

I sneak a glance at the hockey god sharing my space, wondering how a sitcom could possibly hold his interest.

He probably doesn't understand what they're saying.

"See, Max is the sarcastic one who—" I begin to explain, but Tristan cuts me off with a soft kiss to my forehead, his lips lingering a beat too long against my skin.

"I got it, sunshine. You watch, I'm good just chillin' here with you." His dark eyes sparkle with sincerity.

My foolish heart stutters again, as if his smallest gesture of affection is a breakaway goal that catches me off-guard every time.

I'm in trouble and I know it. Falling for Tristan Bane is a penalty I can't afford.

I sit up straighter, putting some welcome distance between us. "So...I've been meaning to ask. About your dating history—"

"Don't take me back to history class. I'm focused on the present." He winks, flashing that knee-melting grin. "On you."

Oh no, mister, you're not smooth-talking your way out of this one.

"But the blogs say you're quite the player. Breaking hearts all over town. What's the real story there?"

"What?" Tristan shrugs, unconcerned. "I don't know what that's about. But when it comes to women I dated prior, I liked to keep things casual. It's no big deal, and I was always upfront about it."

"Right, because you're allergic to commitment." I raise a skeptical brow. "Has the word 'girlfriend' ever left your lips before this fake arrangement?"

"Whoa, whoa!" He clutches his chest in mock offense.

"I'll have you know I'm a relationship guru. I've got 'boyfriend material' branded on my hockey pads."

I roll my eyes, but can't hide my smile. "Sure, Casanova."

"Why are you grilling me anyway, Faye? Seems like maybe you're the one scared to catch feelings, not me." Tristan's gaze turns smoldering, pinning me in place. "Every time we kiss, you usually book it out of here like your skates are on fire."

"Excuse me? I am NOT scared! We kissed." My voice drops to a whisper. "We did it in the pool. I'm not scared."

"I initiated it. If you aren't scared of me, prove it then. I dare you." His voice is pure challenge dipped in honey. That sinful mouth quirks up, begging to be shut up.

Indignation and challenge swells in my chest.

This isn't high school. I shouldn't pettily jump into situations just to prove a man wrong.

That's how I ended up in some of the relationships that almost ruined me.

But when he puts it that way…

I launch myself at Tristan, capturing his tempting lips with my own. A stupid effort to wipe that cocky look off his unfairly gorgeous face.

Tristan responds instantly, a low growl rising in his throat as he pulls me flush against the solid heat of his body.

I lose myself in the demanding crush of his mouth, in wandering hands that skim and tease.

His clever tongue dances with mine, and I all but melt into his arms, dizzy from lack of oxygen.

Or maybe from the sheer intoxicating rush that is Tristan when he kisses like the world is ending.

We surface for air, foreheads pressed together, panting in sync. Tristan looks as dazed as I feel. "Wow. That was…"

"Amazing," I finish for him with a breathless laugh. "No penalty minutes required."

His chuckle mingles with mine, and I know I'm playing with fire, but I can't bring myself to care.

Not when Tristan keeps looking at me like I'm the only goal he wants to score.

And I'd happily play along, even if it means I'm sure to get burned when the final buzzer sounds on this make-believe romance.

Once again, his big hand cups my cheek.

This should be my cue. To leave. To protect my heart.

Instead, I lean in for another kiss. And it's just as incredible.

His tongue slicks over mine, winning a battle I don't even bother fighting. With a loud moan, I angle my neck to deepen the kiss.

Hunger replaces blood, shooting through my veins in a rush of lust that I'm unfamiliar with.

Tristan loops his fingers into my damp hair, pulling me onto him with a groan. My breasts press against his rock hard chest, melting into the ridges of his hot skin.

Even through his shirt that I'm wearing, I can feel the wild beat of his heart against my pebbled nipples.

Something is wrong with me. I'm...addicted.

His mouth moves from my mouth with skill, tracing a heated path along my jawline and down my neck.

The spot between my thighs clenches, still slick with my orgasm by the pool. The sound of a tortured moan overrides the laughter from the TV.

And in a startling moment of realization, it clicks. It's me. I'm the one making those sounds!

"You're so needy." Tristan pulls back with a chuckle, glancing between us. "It's not even been an hour, and you're already wet."

I'm pleasurably aware of his throbbing length below me. It sends pulses through his shorts, past my panties and all over my pussy.

Following his gaze, a wet, dark spot between us calls to me even in the dim lighting.

Entranced, I rock against him, digging my heat harder into his length.

His lips part in an almost feral groan. "Shit, Faye. If you know you're going to stop me, do it now. Please."

I look into his eyes. Black like the ocean on a stormy night.

Control and recklessness wage a battle over his features, and I can feel his hands clenching and unclenching around my waist.

A part of me feels powerful. Right now. In this moment, he's under my control. Tristan Bane is at my mercy. But the crazy part is, I'm at his mercy too.

Never in my life have I felt like this. Sex was never a moment of pleasure. It used to feel like duty. But not with Tristan.

Apart from lust, I can see his hope. His desire to please me.

And this once, I'll let myself go. "Don't stop. I want you to take me. Make me feel goo—"

His mouth swallows the rest of my words as he gently flips me over onto my back. One warm hand slips underneath my shirt, cupping my right breast in a tight grip.

A shot of pleasure dashes through my bones and yet another moan of joy slips from my lips into his.

"Tell me when you want me to stop," his deep voice growls between my explicit moans.

Not if. When.

He's so sure I'm going to ask him to stop. If the feeling that's coupled tight at the base of my spine is anything to go by, he's in for a long ride.

Every pun intended.

My brain is already surfing in the clouds by the time his hands move again.

One on my nipple. The other sliding through my slick folds. Right as the heat of his incoming fingers hits my clit, he stops.

His other hand gets more intense, twisting my nipple with just enough friction to send a fog of white across my sight.

A husky groan mingles with his pleased chuckle as I buck violently against him, sending his fingers right where I wanted them.

His index finger slides straight into my pussy and the other taps a fast rhythm over my clit.

"Should I stop?" Tristan asks, his glistening lips pulled into a fake pout.

"Please, no," I whimper, rocking rapidly onto his fingers.

Tristan doesn't need guidance. Doesn't need a helping hand around a pussy. And he proves it, inserting another finger that lands right on the perfect spot.

The spot that most men chase all their lives.

The spot that most women know exist but can never seem to find. G marks the spot, and Tristan digs in like a pirate, thrusting his fingers in and out.

"Yes, I know you're close. Stop overthinking it, Faye. It's okay to feel pleasure."

He lets out a low growl of approval, swallowing my orgasmic screams with another kiss.

"Oh god. Tristaaaaannn!"

With one final tap on my clit, I go off like a gunshot, limbs locked in toe-curling pleasure.

The orgasm is more intense than any of the ones I've barely managed to give myself over the years. It's heated. It's cathartic. Above all, it's amazing.

The next minute feels like an hour. An hour of me repeatedly clenching and unclenching around Tristan's thrusting fingers.

His movements don't falter, prolonging and milking my orgasm for all its worth.

With strangled gasps, my body finally remembers how to work again. I pull him into a hug, our lips melting into a kiss.

My sanity begins to return and I blink slowly, taking in Tristan's pleased smile. His fingers slow to a teasing stroke that makes me shiver and spasm.

"Stooo—stoppp."

He does, leaning back to admire his handiwork. His eyes darken even more at the sight of my quivering lips and his cock pushes against his shorts with rapid throbs.

"You're so beautiful, Faye. So fucking beautiful."

Heat floods over my skin until I feel like a turkey right before Thanksgiving dinner.

"Let's con...let's continue," I stutter, avoiding his coal-black eyes.

Faye. You're out of your goddamned mind!

"It's fine. I don't want to rush you," Tristan insists, rolling off me with a huff.

Confused and my legs still shaking, I point at his erection shyly. "Then, what about that?"

"I'll handle it later."

The oddity of the situation dawns on me. How come I'm the one pushing for sex.

My insides clench again, and I can feel my wetness drip down my thighs.

Want. Need. Desire.

Call it what you want, but I need him inside me.

Every inch of my skin is aflame with pleasure and an intensity I'm not quite sure how to handle.

Tristan leans back against the couch, shamelessly adjusting himself through his pants. My cheeks flame with heat as I look down at him.

With a sudden burst of strange confidence, I lunge forward, lips pressing against his mouth.

A strangled sound escapes him, and his fingers twine in my curls, giving them a gentle tug.

The force on my hair shoots from my tingling scalp down to my pulsing pussy, forcing out a drawn out moan from my lips.

"You've got to stop if you don't want me to fuck you, Faye," Tristan repeats harshly for clarity, his voice low and rough.

My right hand slides down to the bulge beneath his pants. It twitches into my palm, like a living thing with a lustful mind of its own.

"That is exactly what I want."

After that, everything becomes a blur. Me on his lap again.

His hands and lips spread in a dance over my body. His tongue flicks and licks at delicate parts of my skin, whisking me away to a whole new world of pleasure.

He leaves me only for a second to reach for a tiny drawer attached to his round coffee table.

My body pulses with both pleasure and warning bells. A shiny pack of condoms comes apart in his shaky fingers, depositing a metallic square onto my lap.

The sharp edges sting my skin painfully as I pick it up and deposit it back into his waiting palm. "Do you need help with it?"

"No. I've got this. I'm afraid if you set as much as a finger on my shaft, I'll blow."

The tearing of plastic breaks the silence, and I glimpse a flash of him pulling himself out of his waistband.

His wet tip glistens in the dim lighting before it's covered in the shiny sheath of a white condom.

Tristan shuffles a bit, reclining until I'm right on top of him like a prized bull rider. "Faye, baby. I know you're good with your hands, but can you ride?"

Swallowing thickly, I shimmy closer and closer until my wetness is right above his groin.

My fingers curl around his girth, falling short of a full wrap around.

"Will this fit?"

"I guess, we'll have to try." Tristan groans, pumping twice into my fist before replacing my hand with his. "Wait. I'm close. Just give me a second."

For the next few moments, I watch his temple glisten with sweat. A losing struggle to hold himself back all because of my touch.

Unwilling to let his rational mind take over again, I use his hand as leverage.

My gaze holding his, I sink down, inch by inch until the beginning of another orgasm crests along my spine.

My insides clench around him in a delicious rhythm, and he unleashes a moan that shoots through my body.

My hips ache for movement. So I move.

I lift myself up and down with a slam so hard that we both groan. My ass cheeks slap against his thighs. Over and over and over again.

I ride him hard and fast, matching the rapidly increasing pace of his upward thrusts.

His furrowed brows and parted lips hold me captive. I'm so focused that when my orgasm finally slams into me again, it knocks me forward in surprise.

"Oh, Tristan," I scream, spasming against him in what feels like an endless crash of pleasure.

His upward thrusts continue, hands branding a tight grip into the soft flesh of my ass.

Groans and grunts fill my ears like a man in pain. But I know he's fine.

This is far from pain. I trail a feverish kiss onto his neck, sucking on his warm skin until he gives a final thrust.

"Fucking hell, Faye. I'm cumming. I'm cumming!"

Spurts of warmth shoot through me, stopping halfway in what is probably the condom.

We remain like that for the next five minutes, luxuriating in post-orgasmic bliss, hearts pounding against each other's.

A sleepy haze pulls me under, aided by the soft weight of Tristan's palm on the back of my head. Another realization bangs through my satiated mind.

I, Faye Williams, am so screwed in more ways than one.

CHAPTER 8

TRISTAN

Early morning sunlight seeps through the cracks in the blinds, draping itself across my bed in a warm caress.

My palm glides over rumpled sheets, seeking the luscious curves that writhed beneath me mere hours ago.

But the space beside me is cold, empty.

Humming sounds drift from the kitchen, accompanied by an orchestra of sizzling, clanking, and the rich aroma of brewing coffee.

Curious, I roll out of bed and tug on a pair of sweats, padding barefoot down the hall.

The scene in my kitchen steals the air from my lungs.

Faye's standing at the stove, her back to me as she flips pancakes with expert precision.

She's wearing one of my old hockey jerseys, the fabric skimming the tops of her thighs and leaving her long, toned legs on full display.

Her untamed crimson curls are piled atop her head in a haphazard bun.

Pots bubble, skillets crackle, and Faye...Faye dances. Her hips sway to some internal rhythm as she hums under her breath, slender fingers flying over an army of mixing bowls.

Beautiful. Captivating. And she has no damn clue.

As I watch, she dips a pinky into a bowl of creamy batter, popping it between her rosebud lips.

Her eyes drift closed, and she emits a groan of pleasure that shoots straight to my groin.

I must have made a sound, because her eyes fly open. She whirls to face me, cheeks flushing prettily.

"Oh! Tristan. I didn't hear you come down." Her gaze darts to my bare chest before skittering away, and a smug thrill zips through me.

"Morning, Red." I prop a shoulder against the doorframe, not bothering to hide my smirk.

"What are you up to here, besides putting on one hell of a show?" I waggle my eyebrows.

Faye rolls her expressive blue eyes, but I catch the hint of a smile tugging at her lips.

"Get your mind out of the gutter, you animal. I'm recipe testing." She gestures to the counters, every inch covered in flour and produce and bowls of colorful goop. "Breakfast is the most important meal of the day, and I'm on a mission to revamp my cafe's morning menu."

I push off the door, sauntering closer.

"Oh yeah? And just what scrumptious surprises does Chef Faye have in store for the hungry masses?"

I reach past her for a mug and fill it with coffee, not-so-accidentally brushing her hip. She sucks in a sharp breath.

"Plenty, if you think your belly can handle it." The challenge in her tone hooks me behind the navel, reeling me in.

"Sweetheart, there isn't a dish you could throw at me that I can't handle." I bring my mug to my lips, holding her gaze over the rim as I take a slow sip. "Lay it on me."

And lay it on me she does. For the next hour, Faye serves up a dizzying array of sweet and savory breakfast concoctions.

Fluffy banana pancakes dripping with dark rum syrup. Cheesy scallion hash brown waffles crowned with silky poached eggs. Buttery blueberry scones that practically melt on the tongue.

I eat with gusto, groaning and nodding and occasionally offering suggestions, which Faye accepts with gleaming eyes.

Watching her in her element, her quicksilver mind and nimble hands crafting edible art, makes my chest feel too small for my ribs.

She's a fucking marvel. A prickly, contrary, beautiful marvel. How did I get so damn lucky?

"All right, last one." Faye brandishes a plate with a flourish. "Lemon ricotta pancakes with honeyed fig butter."

My mouth waters at the golden stack, studded with creamy white pockets and glistening with sticky nectar.

I accept the proffered fork and dig in, my eyes rolling back at the explosion of flavors—tart lemon, rich cheese, jammy sweetness.

It's like summer sunshine and a snowy cabin morning all at once, cozy and bright, naughty and nice.

"Good god, Red. This...I'm *marrying* these pancakes. Forget coffee—this is how I wanna wake up every day for the rest of my life..."

I point my fork at her for emphasis, and a giggle pops out of her. My favorite sound in the whole damn world.

We both ignore the weight of my sentence and move on.

"I'll take that as a compliment, you goof." She snickers, plucking a bite off my plate.

A smudge of lemony filling clings to her upper lip, tantalizingly close to the corner of her mouth. I grin.

"Uh, Red? You got a little somethin'..." I gesture to my own lip, stifling the urge to lean over and lick it clean myself. She makes a face.

"Oops! How embarrassing." Her little pink tongue darts out, swiping once, twice, three times in a futile attempt to catch the errant smear.

I watch, hypnotized, blood rushing south at an alarming rate.

That fucking tongue. If she keeps waving it around like a matador's cape, my red-blooded bull is gonna charge.

I'm moving before I even realize it. Leaning in, I cradle her face between my palms, angling her jaw up.

Her eyes go wide and hazy, breath hitching. My thumbs stroke the delicate curves of her cheeks.

"Here. Let me." And I close the gap, pressing my lips to hers.

Her answering gasp opens her mouth for me, and I slip inside, lapping at that stubborn dab of cream. She melts into me, hands fisting in my shirt.

I pull back reluctantly, my lips tingling. She blinks up at me, dazed.

"I...you...that..." Pink blooms in her cheeks. "We shouldn't. Our agreement..."

I chuckle slowly. "Those flimsy little words? Pretty sure they disintegrated in the heated pool yesterday...and got buried in the sheets last night."

She flushes harder, even as her eyes narrow. "Don't try your charming playboy shtick on me, Casanova. I'm immune, remember?"

Something twists in my chest. "It's not a shtick, Red. Not with you." I sweep a thumb over the plump lip I just sampled. "This, you and me? It's the realest thing I've ever felt."

Something like fear flashes in her eyes, chased by uncertainty. She ducks her head. "Tristan...what we're doing, this fake dating thing...it has an expiration date."

No. Not gonna happen. You're not shaking me that easy, baby.

"Screw the ice. Screw pie dough."

I tip her chin up until those gorgeous blue eyes lock on mine. They glitter with unshed tears.

"Practice starts Monday, but I'm ready to hang up my skates for good if it means I get to keep tasting your pancakes every morning."

As soon as the words leave my mouth, I realize they're true.

This infuriating, intoxicating woman has me wrapped so tight around her flour-dusted fingers, I'd walk away from everything I've ever known or worked for just to make her flash that dimpled grin my way.

She pushes away, hugging herself. I clench my fists against the urge to yank her back. "You don't mean that."

I growl in frustration. "The hell I don't."

Scrubbing a hand down my face, I force my voice to be gentle.

"Look, Faye. I know we started out playing pretend for the cameras. But somewhere along the line, it got real for me." I risk a step, then another, until I'm close enough to feel her heat. "You slayed the beast, baby. Tamed the wild playboy. I'm all in, for real, for keeps."

She looks up at me, eyes searching. I let her see it all—the longing, the devotion, the fear. My soul, laid bare.

After a moment that stretches into eternity, she sighs. "I want to believe you, Tristan. But I've been burned before." A sheen of moisture glazes her eyes. "Guys like you...they don't go for girls like me. Not for keeps."

Red-hot rage boils my blood at the defeated slump of her shoulders.

It burns for whoever made this vibrant goddess doubt her place in my arms, my bed, my life.

I want to hunt them down and pulverize them into nothing.

I reach for her, gratified when she lets me gather her close.

"Forget those assholes, sweetheart. They didn't deserve to breathe your air." I skim my hands down her spine, up her sides. "I'm gonna erase every memory of any jerk who made you feel less than the queen you are."

She shivers, pressing closer. "And how do you plan to do that?"

I flash her a wolfish grin. "Why, by worshiping your body until the only name on your lips is mine." I scoop her up, my hulking form dwarfing her petite one. And then I'm kissing her, my mouth slanting over hers with a desperation that borders on possession.

She gasps against my lips, her fingers tangling in my hair as she pulls me closer.

I groan, low and rough, my tongue delving into the sweet recesses of her mouth.

She tastes like sugar and spice and everything nice, a heady combination that makes my head spin and my blood sing.

I place her onto the table, scattering plates and cutlery in my haste to get closer.

She wraps her legs around my waist, her heels digging into the small of my back as she arches into me.

I trail kisses down the column of her throat, my teeth scraping over the delicate skin. She whimpers, her head falling back to give me better access. "Tristan," she gasps, her fingers clenching in my hair. "Please..."

I pull back, my breath coming in harsh pants. "Please what, baby? Tell me what you want."

She looks up at me, her eyes glazed with desire. "I want you. All of you."

I groan, my forehead falling to rest against hers. "Damn, Faye. You have no idea what you do to me."

She smiles, slow and wicked. "Then show me. Make me feel good, Tristan. Make me forget about everything but you."

I growl, low and rough, before capturing her mouth in a bruising kiss. My hands skim down her sides, tugging at the hem of her shirt until she lifts her arms, letting me pull it over her head. I suck in a sharp breath, my eyes drinking in the sight of her, all creamy skin and soft curves.

She's wearing a simple cotton bra, the pink fabric straining against the lush swells of her breasts.

"Beautiful," I murmur, my fingers tracing the edge of the lacy cups. "So fucking beautiful."

She flushes, her skin pinkening under my gaze. "Tristan..."

But I'm already unhooking her bra, letting it fall to the floor as I palm her breasts in my hands.

She arches into my touch, her nipples pebbling against my palms.

I lower my head, taking one dusky peak into my mouth.

She cries out, her fingers tangling in my hair as I lick her with my tongue, my teeth scraping over the sensitive flesh.

"Oh god," she gasps, her hips rocking against mine. "Don't stop. Please don't stop."

I have no intention of stopping. Not now, not ever. I want to worship every inch of her, to show her with my hands and my mouth just how precious she is to me.

I trail kisses down her stomach, my tongue dipping into her navel. She squirms beneath me, her breath coming in shallow pants.

I hook my fingers in the waistband of her panties, tugging them down her legs until she's bare before me. I groan at the sight of her, all smooth skin and glistening flesh.

"Tristan," she whimpers, her hips lifting in silent invitation. "Please..."

I press a kiss to the inside of her thigh, my breath ghosting over her most sensitive flesh. "Please what, baby? Tell me what you need."

She looks down at me, her eyes dark with desire. "I need you. Inside me. Now."

I grin, slow and wicked. "As the lady wishes."

CHAPTER 9

FAYE

Strong arms band around me, Tristan's warmth seeping into my skin through the thin cotton of his shirt as he carries me down the hall.

My heart hammers frantically against my ribs, anticipation and fear warring for dominance in my stomach.

But then Tristan lays me on the bed with a gentleness that steals my breath, his inky gaze soft and scorching all at once as it roams over my sprawled form.

His large hands skim my sides, igniting currents of electricity that dance along my nerve endings.

"Fuck, Red. You're so fucking gorgeous, sprawled out all pretty for me like this."

His gruff words lodge in my wetness, stroking the flickering flames of my desire.

Maybe...maybe it's okay to feel good, to be cherished...by him.

"But we're just getting started. I'm going to make you fall to pieces on my cock next."

Before my lust-drunk brain can process the filthy promise in those words, he's rolling me beneath him, his thighs nudging mine wider.

His cock, thick and searing, parts my tender folds, stretching me, filling me.

My back arches off the mattress, a ragged gasp lodged in my throat.

So full...he's so deep, splitting me open, touching places inside me I didn't know existed.

My nails dig into the rigid muscles of his back as he starts to move, each powerful thrust sending pleasure zinging straight to my core.

"Fuck, you're tight...squeezing me like a vice." Tristan's voice is a guttural rasp in my ear, his hips churning in a rhythm as old as time. "I'm not gonna last, baby...you feel so damn perfect."

I can only moan in response, my thighs falling open in wanton invitation.

Our bodies move in synchronized bliss, skin slapping, breaths mingling, my needy cries twining with his harsh grunts.

That familiar tension coils in my core once more, pulling me closer and closer to the razor's edge.

"Tristan...oh fuck..." I'm out of it, lost to the feel of him pounding into my willing body.

"That's it, Red. Just let it go, baby..." His filthy words are my undoing.

My orgasm slams into me like a freight train, my head thrashing on the pillow as I shatter in his arms.

Colors burst behind my eyelids, electric currents sizzling through my veins.

Tristan follows me over the edge with a hoarse roar, his powerful body going taut as a bowstring above me.

I feel the hot rush of his release painting my insides, branding me, marking me as his.

Not like he needs to at this point.

★★★

February teases into March with a faint warmth, turning the arena parking lot into a maze of melted slush and puddles.

I pick my way carefully across the melting ice in my new boots—a gift from Tristan after one too many near-falls at public events.

The past month has taught me the rhythm of practice days.

How to time my arrival during water breaks so the paparazzi can get their 'candid' couple shots without disrupting the team.

Which seats offer the best angle for the 'devoted girlfriend' photos that keep appearing in sports blogs.

In less than five minutes, I'm bundled up in the stands of the Blizzard's practice rink as usual, Tristan's giant water bottle clutched in my mittened hands like a talisman.

I watch in awe as he glides across the ice, his movements powerful and graceful in equal measure.

The puck dances across the blade of his stick, his skates leaving curling trails behind him with each twisting turn.

He's in his element out here, a king on this frozen court.

It's mesmerizing, the way he seems to anticipate each play before it happens, his body always exactly where it needs to be.

Just like it was last night.

"Damn, Bane is on fire today," a voice says from my left, startling me out of my reverie.

I glance over to see a petite brunette smiling at me, her hazel eyes sparkling.

"Hi, I'm Stella, by the way. Slick's better half. I'm sorry it took this long but welcome to the WAGs club."

I blink, suddenly feeling out of my depth. The ladies usually kept to themselves on the other side. "The what club now?"

Stella laughs, the sound bright and infectious. "Wives and Girlfriends. Or in some cases, Boyfriends. We're the poor souls who put up with these hockey-obsessed man-children."

She nods toward the ice, where Tristan is currently trading barbs with a hulking blonde in a red practice jersey.

"That one is mine, Lucas Martinez, but you can call him Slick," Stella confides, her nose wrinkling. "And there, right next to each other are Doc and Diesel. You'll be seeing a lot of them."

I will?

I doubt it. Surely, when our so-called relationship comes to an end, so will all this. It's been a month of bliss but all good things will come to an end.

The shrill chirp of an incoming text jolts me from my heavy thoughts.

Blowing out a breath, I dig my phone from the depths of my Michael Kors crossbody—another gift from Tristan that I just couldn't refuse.

Squinting at my cracked screen, I see Ben's name flashing urgently. Honestly, that boy's timing...

I swipe to open his message, bracing for whatever mini-crisis has sent my baby-faced delivery guy into conniptions this time.

Ben:

Boss-lady!!!!

Ben:

Cafe is crazy. Send back-up! Or sedatives! Or a priest for last rites!

Despite my tangled emotions, a grin tugs at the corners of my mouth. Leave it to my excitable man-child of an employee to inject some much-needed levity.

Faye:

Cool your jets, Benji. What's the haps?

Ben:

The HAPS is, we're up to our eyeballs in thirsty hockey fans. Again.

This Tristan Bane effect is no joke, Boss.

I groan aloud, tipping my head back. The lovey-dovey pictures from yesterday's charity event worked crazy well.

Blowing out a breath, I tap out a response, my thumbs flying over the screen.

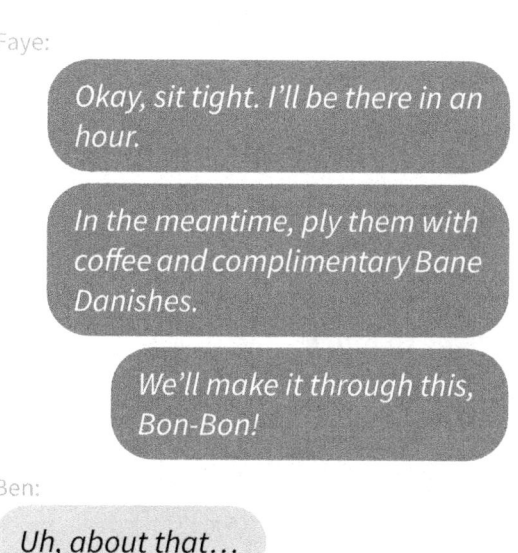

Faye:

> Okay, sit tight. I'll be there in an hour.

> In the meantime, ply them with coffee and complimentary Bane Danishes.

> We'll make it through this, Bon-Bon!

Ben:

> Uh, about that...

Oh no. I know that tone. It's the same sheepish inflection he gets when confessing he "accidentally" locked himself in the walk-in fridge again.

Faye:

> Rip the Band-Aid off, bucko.
> What happened?

Ben:

> Well...we maybe kinda sorta
> RAN OUT OF DANISHES TEN
> MINUTES AGO.

> And scones.

> And muffins.

> And those cherry tarts Tristan
> likes so much.

> We're down to one lonely
> cruller and half a bag of
> Splenda.

For a beat, I can only gape at my phone, my jaw hanging somewhere in the vicinity of my knees.

Then an incredulous giggle bubbles up my throat.

Unbelievable. My adorable little breakfast nook that I was so worried about had been stripped barer than Old Mother Hubbard's cupboard.

Faye:

> ...I don't know whether to high-five you or faint.

> Okay, new plan. Brew a fresh pot of Sumatran dark roast.

> Pray to the pastry gods for mercy.

> I'll be there ASAP to relieve you.

> DON'T DIE ON ME, BENJI!

Ben:

> You're a lifesaver, Boss-Lady!

> And I just saw pictures of you at the rink online.

> You guys are cute.

Heat floods my cheeks, staining them a vivid crimson to rival my hair. I sink down into my puffy coat, a flustered huff escaping my lips.

I'm saved from having to respond by the sharp blast of the coach's whistle, signaling the end of practice.

The players glide to a stop, their chests heaving, and their faces flushed with exertion.

Tristan skates over to where I'm sitting, his eyes bright, and his grin infectious. "Hey, Red. Enjoying the show?"

I roll my eyes, but I can't quite suppress my answering smile. "Oh, you know. Just admiring the view."

His grin widens, his gaze raking over me in a way that makes my blood heat. "Funny, I was just thinking the same thing."

Before I can formulate a response, he's leaning over the boards and pulling me into a kiss.

His lips are cold from the ice, but his tongue is hot as it tangles with mine, sending shivers racing down my spine.

I can hear the whoops and catcalls of his teammates, the giggling whispers of the WAGs behind me.

It never gets old and I don't mind it. In this moment, there's only Tristan. His taste, his touch, the way he makes me feel like the center of his universe.

He pulls back far too soon, his breath mingling with mine in the space between us.

"Wait for me in the car?" he murmurs, his voice low and intimate. "I'll be out in ten."

I nod, not trusting myself to speak.

He presses a kiss to my forehead, his lips curving into a smile against my skin, before skating away to join his rowdy teammates.

I gather my things on autopilot, my mind still hazy with the drugging heat of Tristan's kiss.

I'm so lost in my own head, in the giddy swirl of my thoughts, that I don't register the voices at first.

The murmur of sound that seems to be growing louder with each step I take.

It's not until I push through the heavy metal door leading to the parking lot that I realize what I'm hearing. What I'm seeing.

Cameras. Dozens of them. Flashing and clicking and whirring like a swarm of mechanical insects.

And in the center of it all, a sea of faces. Eager. Hungry. All turned in my direction.

What on earth…Tristan is usually with me for the rapid fire paps.

"Faye!" a voice calls out, the word sharp and demanding. "Faye Williams! Do you truly love Tristan Bane?"

"It's been a month of bliss," another voice chimes in. "Could this actually be serious?"

"Are there any plans for marriage in the near future?"

The questions keep coming, rapid-fire and relentless. I feel like a deer caught in the headlights, wide-eyed and utterly, completely trapped.

This can't be happening. This can't be real.

But it is. The proof is right there in front of me, in the wall of cameras and microphones and shouted questions.

My private little bubble with Tristan...it's gone. Shattered like a pane of glass, leaving me exposed and vulnerable for all the world to see.

If this is what it's always going to be like dating a celebrity...I'm not sure I want any part of it.

CHAPTER 10

TRISTAN

Buzzzzzz.

I shoot off at the sound of the buzzer. The sharp bite of cold air burns my lungs as I skate across the ice, my blades cutting lines into the worn surface.

Blood pumps in my ears, nearly drowning out the crowd's roar.

This is what I live for. The rush, the thrill, pushing myself to the limit. Nothing else matters when I'm out here. It's just me, my stick, and the game.

A flash catches my eye—their offense, Donaldson, weaving through the neutral zone with the puck.

I angle toward him, muscles coiling. Just as I'm about to check him, a familiar swirl of red hair catches my attention.

Faye.

She's in the stands, her hair a bright spot of color among the sea of Blizzard fans in jerseys.

Even from here, I can see my number on her chest, my name is definitely printed on her back. The the thought sends a rush of satisfaction through me.

Mine.

The distraction costs me. Donaldson slips past, and the crowd's jeers fill the air.

"Bane! What the hell was that?"

Coach's shout snaps me back to reality.

Gritting my teeth, I refocus, welcoming the burn in my legs. It stabs in my knees, burning a painful heat through the carefully wrapped tape beneath my uniform.

I know that the game won't wait, and I can't let my team down. Not when we're this close to the playoffs.

The minutes blur into a mix of sweat, aching muscles, and adrenaline. We're locked in a brutal match, the scoreboard reflecting our tie.

My teammates are flagging, exhaustion pulling at them. We need a miracle.

"Yo, Blade!" Diesel, my forward yells, his voice rough. "Pull some magic. Otherwise, we're buying drinks for these clowns."

A grin tugs at my mouth behind my mask. "Over my dead body, Connor. Let's do this."

Ignoring the burn, I push harder against their offense, my skates slicing over the ice. My stick swings, hitting the puck with a hard crack.

The crowd's eyes are on me as I race toward the opposing goal.

Time slows, the noise fading except for my heartbeat.

I fake left, then right, handling the puck with smooth control. The goalie crouches, his stick ready.

Not today, buddy. This puck's heading straight for the back of your net.

I snap my wrists at the last second, and the puck flies through the air, hitting the net.

SCORE.

The arena erupts, and my teammates swarm around me, pounding my back. We still need one more to tie, but this goal has fired everyone up.

I spot Faye in the crowd, her face lit with a wide smile. She's on her feet, cheering. Pride swells in my chest.

We line up for the face-off, sticks hovering over the puck.

The crowd buzzes with excitement, and I can feel the tension from my teammates. We have less than a minute left to tie the game.

The whistle blows, and the puck drops. Sticks clash and bodies collide as we fight for control and defense.

Out of the corner of my eye, I see Donaldson break away with the puck. Our eyes meet for a split second, a silent challenge passing between us.

Not with my team, jerk.

I wait on his path, ready to knock him down. But just as he's about to make contact, my right leg seizes, pain exploding up my knee.

The world tilts as black spots dance in my vision. The crowd gasps and my body thuds against the ice.

"TRISTAN!"

Faye's panicked voice cuts through everything. Shame rises in my throat.

Of all times for my leg to fail...

"Bane! You alright?"

Slick's gruff voice pulls me back, and I blink up at his blonde hair spilling through his helmet and over his face, creased with worry and frustration.

Get up. Don't lay here like a fool in front of Faye. In front of everyone. Move.

I grit my teeth and force myself to stand, lifting a hand to acknowledge the crowd. I have to save face.

Doc claps my shoulder, his grip tight and voice tiny. "Good job, Blade. Walk it off. We'll get the docs to check you after the game."

I nod, unable to speak. Across the ice, Donaldson smirks, clearly pleased. Anger blazes through me, numbing the pain.

The game speeds up, the seconds ticking down like a bomb. Every step is agony, but I'm not letting the Boston Cheetah's win.

I catch a wild pass from Slick, controlling the puck. He knows I need this win.

The defenders close in, but I duck and twist, pushing through the pain. With one last burst, I speed toward the net, the noise of the crowd fading to a dull hum.

One shot. One chance.

I fire the puck, pouring all my frustration into the shot. It sails through the crowd of players and lands in the top corner of the net.

AND THE SNOWFIELD BLIZZARDS WIN!

The arena erupts, my teammates shouting and pounding my back. Even Coach cracks a smile.

But all I see is Faye, tears glistening on her cheeks as she grins at me. My heart stumbles, then steadies.

I skate over to her, leaning my stick on the boards.

She grabs my jersey. "Tristan! Are you okay? When you went down, I thought my heart stopped."

I press my forehead to hers, my gloves framing her face. "I'm good, Red. More than good. We did it! Playoffs, here we come!"

Her squeal of joy makes me grin, and she pulls me into a hard kiss. The edge of my helmet bites into my face, but I couldn't care less.

I've got a giddy hellcat molded to my front and victory fizzing in my blood. Life is great.

***

My euphoria lasts all through my post-game shower and change, buoying my steps as I limp through the hallways.

A few of the guys throw me hearty backslaps and bro-nods, their faces ruddy with the flush of hard-won triumph.

"Ayyyyy, Casanova!" Matty, one of the rookies, wolf-whistles as I round the corner. "Your ass is blowing up online, stud. Your little smooch is trending on Twitter again. Hashtag PuckBunnyGoals."

I roll my eyes, fighting a smirk. Let the gossipy buzzards yap. I don't give a flying fuck who knows Faye's mine.

In fact, I want the world to see I'm spoken for, off the market, one-hundred-percent devoted to my sassy baker.

I'll be her hockey boyfriend till they put me in the ground.

I'm so tangled up in sappy thoughts of Faye, I almost miss the usual buzz of voices up ahead.

Cameras flash like lightning bugs outside the double doors of the arena, the exit sign winking mockingly.

Squaring up, I arrange my face into an expressionless mask while looking around for my girlfriend.

But before I can find her, a small hand slips into mine, fragile and smooth. The hand of my little baker.

I glance down to find Faye peering up at me, worry creasing her brow.

Even wrung out and anxious, she's the most beautiful thing I've ever seen.

"Babe? Why do you look like you're marching to your own firing squad?" Her husky murmur caresses my overheated skin, settling me like nothing else.

I blow out a breath, giving her fingers a gentle squeeze.

"Fucking paps have the joint surrounded. No doubt gagging to pick apart my performance and grill me about that fall. Goddamn bottom-feeding scavengers."

Faye purses her lips, genuine concern softening her pixie face. She gets it.

Weeks and weeks of pushing through paparazzi questions with me has created a shared empathy.

"Oh, honey." Rising on her toes, she brushes a fleeting kiss over my stubbled jaw. "Don't sweat the small stuff, yeah? You were a beast out there. Let the armchair bandits chirp. We both know you left it all on the ice."

"Thank you." I flash her a crooked grin, tugging her closer. "You always know just what to say."

Her eyes sparkle impishly, the beginnings of a smirk twitching her lips.

"What can I say? I'm an amazing Tristan Whisperer. Now let's go face the firing squad, soldier. With me on your arm, those yappy microphones don't stand a chance."

Her words are confident but I can feel her hand trembling in mine.

Her previous encounters with paps had been ripped straight out of a horror novel. But here she is, trying to make me feel better.

With our heads held high and fingers locked, Faye and I push through the doors, the frozen night air stinging our cheeks.

Just as I predicted, we're instantly bombarded by questions and popping flashes.

"Bane! Bane, over here! Why did you fall? Looked like you were favoring it in the third."

"Is it true you've been playing through a nagging injury this season? Why keep it under wraps?"

"Tristan, can you comment on the rumors that you've been clashing with Coach behind closed doors?"

What?

Panic flutters in my gut, but I shove it down ruthlessly. Show no weakness. I open my mouth, ready to bust out the patented Tristan Bane Press Charm.

But just as I'm about to pour on the smarm, another voice rises above the clamor, dripping saccharine venom.

"Tristan! Over here!" A bony elbow jabs through the throng, followed by a helmet of platinum hair and a shark-toothed smile.

"Brooke Hart, Inside Edition. Care to comment on the allegations that you proposed to your ex, Julianna earlier today? She just posted a picture of it on her Instagram."

The blood in my veins turns to antifreeze. *Julianna. Fucking Julianna and her fucking mental issues.*

I already know where the photo came from.

For a moment, I'm transported back six months ago during a drinking game. Me, her Tiffany ring in hand, asking her to marry me as a punishment for losing.

And now, that moment is about to destroy the best thing to ever happen to me.

Through the screeching static in my ears, I can hear Faye's hitched gasp, feel her fingers trembling against my clammy palm.

Before I can form a coherent sentence, the rabid wolverine that is the reporter thrusts her Fox-News face into my personal space, her sugary smile doing nothing to soften the malice in her eyes.

"Come clean, Captain Heartbreaker. Is the baker just a slice on the side? Does your REAL fiancée know you're playing house with the proletariat?"

The syrupy push in her voice finally snaps me out of my infuriated daze.

Drawing myself up, I fix her with the iciest death-glare in my arsenal, revulsion curdling in my gut.

"First of all, get your fake nose out of my face, Brook. I don't want to catch whatever communicable insanity you're harboring. Second?"

I twine my arm firmly around Faye's rigid shoulders, reeling her into my side. Her warmth bleeds into me, lending me strength.

"Faye is my GIRLFRIEND. The only reason I haven't put a ring on her finger is because she hasn't said yes yet. But rest assured, our 'playing house' is built on a foundation so solid, you and your forked fucking tongue couldn't chip it with a sandblaster."

Brooke's nostrils flare, two livid splotches of color burning her cheeks. But I don't spare her another thought, too busy guiding a silent Faye through the clamoring crush of bodies.

We make it to my Rover on autopilot, Faye stiff and distant in the passenger seat as she scrolls through her phone.

The moment in my memory is splashed across her screen in vivid HD.

As soon as the doors slam shut, I reach for her, apologies crowding my throat. But she holds up a trembling hand, pain etching deep grooves around her mouth.

"Don't. Answer this first. Is the picture real?" Her voice cracks on the single syllable, fissures spider-webbing my heart.

"Yes, but—"

"Just...drive. Please."

Helpless frustration boils in my blood, but I comply, steering us through darkened streets gilded with patches of melting snow.

Neither of us breathes a word as I navigate back roads made unfamiliar by anguish and gnawing fear.

I'm losing her.

The tight bond we forged in sweat-soaked sheets and laughter-filled kitchens is fraying with every mile.

All because my past is a snake pit even Indiana Fucking Jones can't escape.

After an eternity, I pull into my driveway. The familiar sight of my hulking mansion provides cold comfort.

Faye has her door open before I cut the engine, her boots scraping against the icy cement. "I'll be gone before you return from practice tomorrow."

What right do I actually have to beg her to stay?

None.

CHAPTER 11

FAYE

It's an ungodly hour, even for a baker. Yet, I find myself slouched over the kitchen island, listlessly dragging a spoon through a tub of Ben and Jerry's.

My phone buzzes with a reminder.

Stella:

> *Dinner with the team. PS-Wear matching colors with Tristan.*

A scoff rips out of my lips. The notification for the team dinner for players and WAG's that I've attended for the past seven weeks suddenly feels like a joke.

Four days.

It's been four days since I walked out of Tristan's life, since that mystery figure skater blew up our bliss with a single post.

I can't even find it in me to look her up on Instagram.

God, how pathetic can you get, Faye? Crying into your ice cream at three a.m. like a cliché from a Cathy comic...

A jangle of keys at the front door jolts me from my mopey introspection.

I hastily swipe at my cheeks, hoping my blotchy complexion will blend with the shadows. No such luck.

Cara stumbles over the threshold in yesterday's scrubs, her blonde hair a bird's nest above exhausted eyes. One look at my sorry state, and those dark eyes narrow.

"Aw, honey." Her voice is sympathetic as she makes a beeline for the coffee pot. "Still riding the Heartbreak Express, huh?"

I can only sniffle in response, jabbing viciously at a frozen chunk of fudge.

Cara sighs, plopping down across from me and snagging the tub. She takes a hefty scoop, humming appreciatively.

"Babe, I know you're hurting, but this…" She waves her spoon at my stained shirt and lank ponytail. "This is officially Defcon Pathetic."

Hurt spears through me, sharp and icy. Shoving away from the couch, I pace to the window, hugging myself. "Gee, thanks so much for the pep talk. I'll just flip the old Happy Switch and get over the man I…"

Love?

Cara makes a wounded sound, abandoning the ice cream to drape herself over my back like a human Snuggie. "Shit, Faye. I'm sorry. I suck at this whole feelings thing."

Turning in her embrace, I drop my head to her shoulder, dampening her scrub top with my stupid leaky eyeballs. She rocks me gently, smoothing my hair.

"For the record, I think Tristan's an epic douche for jerking you around. You deserve all the happiness. Especially after that asshole, Shaun."

A watery chuckle escapes me. "Thanks, Care Bear."

Pulling back, I swipe my nose on my sleeve, grimacing.

"I just...it all happened so fast, ya know? One minute, I'm a small-town nobody, cheerfully anonymous. Next thing I know, my face is splashed across every gossip site from here to Mars, linked to Tristan "Blade" Bane."

I retrieve my abandoned phone from the counter, opening Instagram with a resigned tap.

"And now...now I'm a walking tabloid headline. Tristan's Tawdry Tart. The Bakery Floozy."

The other woman. The one thing I swore to never become.

***

By the time the grandfather clock in the lobby wheezes eleven tiny chimes, Kiss & Crumble is hopping like a bingo parlor.

Every table is crammed, the booths overflowing with hordes.

A tinkling riot of laughter and gossip bounces off the exposed brick, nearly drowning out Beyoncé crooning through the speakers.

"Holy Taco Tuesday," Ben says by way of greeting. He skids to a halt beside me at the register, swiping a tired wrist across his brow.

"Is it just me, or have we entered an alternate dimension where our humble bakery is the only seller of baked goods in a trillion-mile radius?"

"It's because misery loves company and everyone wants a scoop," I mutter tersely, jabbing the register keys with more force than necessary.

My arm aches from the repetitive scooping and bagging motions, but it's a welcome distraction from the dull throb in my heart.

"Or maybe they just can't stay away from your delicious lemon tarts!" A brash baritone cuts through the chatter, sending my head snapping up fast.

I know that voice.

Oh God...

My heart drops. Standing in my doorway is one of the last people I expected to see.

Connor "Diesel" Thompson stands before me, a human wall of denim, leather, and muscle.

Beside him, Magic and Doc loom like a pair of sculpted bookends, their faces a mix of sheepish and hopeful.

"H-hey guys." I wince at the wobble in my voice, my palms instantly clammy on the countertop. "What, um...what brings you by?"

Are they here to watch and gossip too?

Diesel shifts from one massive booted foot to the other, ducking his chin boyishly.

It's a startlingly vulnerable gesture from a man who looks like he bench-presses Mini Coopers for funsies.

"Well, see, the thing is…" He roughs a paw over his buzz cut, the brown fuzz gleaming like spun gold.

"You haven't been around the rink the last couple days, and the guys…we're suffering from powerful pastry withdrawals."

His sea-green gaze lifts to mine, pleading and contrite.

"Think you could throw your best boys a bone, cinnamon-bun flavored preferably?"

Beside him, Doc and Magic bob their heads in eager agreement, twin sets of Bambi eyes pleading with me.

Talk about a plot twist.

Heaving a sigh, I snag a takeout box and begin filling it with the team's usual: bacon maple scones, lemon poppy seed muffins, cheddar jalapeño bagels.

The familiar routine soothes my jitters, even as my insides burn with hopeless longing. It's not the Blizzards' fault their buddy turned out to be a two-timing philanderer.

Soon, I'm sliding the laden box across the counter, along with a carrier of steaming dark coffee. "There you go, boys. On the house."

"You're an angel, Faye."

Diesel accepts the bounty reverently, cradling it to his barrel chest. But his expression remains troubled, a crease forming between his sandy brows.

"Listen, about Tristan…"

"Don't." I hold up a palm, my throat constricting painfully. "Just...don't. Please."

"He misses you, Faye." Doc's soft interjection lances through me, sharp as a skate blade.

His warm brown eyes brim with sympathy behind wire-rimmed glasses. "Like, he really misses you. Mopes around the locker room sighing, stares at his phone willing it to ring. It's tragic."

I doubt that.

"Good!" The bitter retort bursts out of me, my eyes stinging. "Serves him right, stringing me along while his slinky ex-fiancée waited in the wings. I hope he chokes on the silver spoon she probably feeds him with."

"What? Nah, it's not like that."

Magic's brow furrows, his angular face pinched with confusion. "Jules is ancient history, more than six months ago. Tristan's hook, line, and sinker for you."

"Yeah, well." I blink furiously, wrangling my pesky emotions into submission. "He sure has a funny way of showing it. How did that picture come about?"

For someone like Tristan to go down on one knee, he must have loved her. Not like...love.

185

Probably why he didn't even make any effort to reach out. No calls, no messages.

She was worth a bended knee but I'm not even worth an apology.

The guys exchange loaded glances, an unspoken conversation flowing between them. Finally, Slick clears his throat, slapping a wad of dollar bills in front of me.

"Just...give him a chance to explain, yeah? I've known Tristan a long time, and I've never seen him twisted up like this. You're special."

Might as well make it a Facebook post and tag Julianna.

Swallowing the jagged lump in my throat, I dredge up a forced smile. "Thanks, guys. I...I appreciate you looking out."

I gently push the money back to him, stepping back both physically and emotionally. "You guys should get those pastries back to the arena. I'll see you around, okay?"

The guys take their cue, filing out with murmured thanks and concerned glances.

Soon, the only evidence of their visit is a lingering whiff of Dior, sausage, axe body spray, and the bitter ache in my chest. Slumping against the register, I stare out at the cafe, my mind a million miles away.

At a mansion with a large indoor pool, strong arms banded around me as a wicked mouth maps my skin...

This makes no sense. I'm no fool. After a day of simmering in my anger, it was pretty clear that something was amiss. But he hasn't even bothered to call.

Almost as if I don't matter.

***

Later, as the listless orange smudge of sunset paints the curtains of my room at home, I collapse face-first onto my bed, one arm flailing blindly for my stuffie.

My hand closes around the worn plush penguin, dragging him to my chest in a stranglehold disguised as a snuggle.

"Oh, Mr. S," I mumble into the threadbare fuzz of his belly, my words muffled. "What am I gonna do? I'm pining over a guy who has probably picked up a new conquest already."

The stuffed penguin's glassy eyes stare back at me, wise and sympathetic. I've been pouring my heart out to him since I was sixteen, and his fuzzy brand of comfort never fails.

Heaving a sigh, I roll onto my back, blinking up at the plaster ceiling. I haul my ass off the bed and stalk to the bathroom, tossing Mr. S over my shoulder.

"The annual baking competition is less than two weeks away, Mr. Scuffington. I need to get my butt in gear and start prepping if I wanna take home that blue ribbon."

I pause midway through yanking my sweaty tee over my head, the spark of an idea taking hold.

"I'll bake my signature spring pie—Lemon Lavender Dreams! Spring is upon us after all."

Chuckling evilly, I shimmy out of my leggings and underwear, cranking up the shower tap. Soon, I'm elbow-deep in a cloud of steam and lemongrass-scented lather, my mind whirring with new recipe ideas.

Humming under my breath, I tip my head forward, relishing the scorching spray pounding my knotted shoulders.

See? This is what you need. A project to focus on. No more moping over a beefcake with magic fingers.

The unbidden memory of calloused hands skating over my skin sends a shiver zipping down my spine that has nothing to do with the shower's fluctuating temperature.

Suddenly, the innocent act of soaping up my curves takes on a whole new meaning as snapshots of moans and groans bombard me in humiliating technicolor.

Tristan's teeth, scraping the vein in my neck as he growls in pleasure...

My fingers, twisting in sweat-damp jet-black hair as he sucks my nipples...

The obscene perfection of his muscled ass flexing as he surges over me, into me...

"Oh God..." A broken moan slips past my lips. Almost helplessly, I trail a trembling hand down my slick body, following the path Tristan's wicked tongue blazed a few nights ago.

My fingers graze the trimmed thatch of curls at the apex of my thighs and my back arches, a sharp gasp rising from my throat.

This is crazy. Insane. You can't just...diddle yourself in the shower like a creeper.

What if Cara hears? What if the neighbors call the cops because the sad girl next door is getting her rocks off at an ungodly decibel?

But even as the majority of my brain scolds and rationalizes, that small, secret part—the part that longs for a pair of midnight eyes and a knowing smirk—drowns out the noise with a hiss.

You need this. Quit overthinking and let yourself feel for one damn second...

I wage a three-second war with my better judgment but it's over before the first volley.

With a breathy sigh, I slide two fingers through the slippery folds of my pussy, my hips rising into the touch.

An answering pulse tightens in my core, hot and achy. Slowly, I begin to circle my swollen clit, the pleasure pain bright as it shoots through my veins.

In my mind, it's not my slim, pruny digits plundering my wet pussy.

It's his. Long, blunt and tan, the pads roughened by a lifetime of stick-handling. He'd stroke me just like this, his touch sure and devastating on my sweet spot...

"Tristan..." His name is a broken sob as I work myself with increasing urgency, my free hand braced on slippery blue tile. Behind my clenched lids, he thrusts into me, all chiseled features and hungry obsidian eyes.

"That's it, Red," he rumbles, breath gusting hotly over the shell of my ear. *"Show me how bad you need it. Drench those fingers, baby. Wish they were mine..."*

"Arghhhh." I come undone with a muffled scream, my knees locking like a vault door.

I can't continue like this.

CHAPTER 12

TRISTAN

Slick:

> Yo. What happened to going soft on women, Blade?

> Your post was brutal.

Tristan:

> Juliana had it coming.

> Leaking that video of her doing drugs is me going easy on her.

Slick:

> Fair enough. What about Faye, though? She's devastated.

> I almost told her you sent us to the cafe.

I'd have broken your nose.

Faye deserves a grand gesture of love. The whole shebang.

Not a half-assed explanation of my philandering ways.

Slick:

Since we're on the topic… remember Anastasia? The hot judge from Compton.

Can I have her now that you're all reformed?

Tristan:

Oh, fuck off.

***

The Snowfield Springs Town Square blooms with bright spring colors, delicate cherry blossoms, and crocuses dotting the awakening earth.

Townsfolk have shed their heaviest winter layers, thick jackets and pastel scarves replacing puffy coats as the March breeze carries the promise of warmer days.

The slightly cold air is alive with the tantalizing scents of cinnamon, nutmeg, and sugar.

I elbow my way through the crowd, craning my neck for a glimpse of crimson curls.

Where is she, dammit?

I take my time weighing the realization that my next conversation with Faye will be for real. A relationship. No lies. No facades.

Also, I feel guilty. The hate campaign against Faye is unbelievable.

From name-calling to sending death threats to her email. I've been getting the morbid notifications too—thanks to that one time when she logged in to check something on my phone.

"Oi! Bane!"

The familiar bellow cuts through the festival chatter.

Hope sparks in my chest but quickly fades when I spot Diesel weaving through the crowd, his massive frame wrapped in a violently purple Kiss and Crumble promotional jacket.

His arms overflow with flat, unassembled cupcake boxes, the pile wobbling precariously as he walks.

"Oh, God." Grinding my molars, I stalk over to my teammate, shouldering through the throng.

"Dude. What the hell are you doing here?"

Diesel just smirks, somehow managing to shrug without dropping his precious cargo.

"Supporting our girl, same as you." He jerks his chin at something over my shoulder. "Turns out we aren't the only ones, either."

I frown, turning to follow his gaze...and I nearly swallow my damn tongue.

There, clustered around a bright yellow booth dripping with glittery streamers, are the Blizzards.

Behind them is a banner that reads: *Kiss and Crumble.*

Slick and Doc lean on the counter, munching neon-frosted cookies while they bicker over a crumpled list.

Matty, our rookie winger, snaps selfies with a group of starry-eyed tweens in 'I love Faye!' shirts. And at the center of it all, like a balding ringmaster...

No way.

"Coach Bates?" I croak, blinking rapidly.

Surely the cinnamon fumes are inducing hallucinations.

There's no way coach is here in all his antisocial glory, at a rinky-dink bake-off, surrounded by giddy civilians.

Coach chooses that moment to lift his head and spot me, bushy brows climbing into his nonexistent hairline.

"Ah, Bane." He beckons me closer with an impatient wave. "Get your tail over here, son."

Jaw unhinged, I comply, weaving through the milling crowd until I reach Faye's booth.

Up close, I can see it's even more bright, strewn with neon posters and glittery knickknacks.

But she isn't here.

Dizzy, I turn to Coach, my voice climbing octaves. "What in the name of Gordie Howe's jockstrap is going on here? Why are you guys accosting Faye's booth like a pack of overripe groupies?"

Coach levels me with a steely gaze, bushy mustache twitching.

"Supporting our girl. She's family now." His expression gentles a fraction. "Poor thing's been running herself ragged after the whole media frenzy."

When did he go from asking me to come clean about the fake relationship to acting like her dad?

I scrub a hand down my face, guilt churning in my gut at the thought of Faye's plight.

"Coach, I swear, it isn't what Faye thinks. That bloodsucking harpy Julianna twisted everything up, made it seem like—"

"Oh, we know, Casanova," Doc pipes up, pushing his glasses up his nose. "Julianna always was a few pucks short of a bucket."

"Yeah, she made it pretty clear back then that she wouldn't let you off her hook," Slick chimes in, dodging the swat I aim at his head.

"I keep telling Faye that too but I think she needs to hear it from you. Girl could crack the whip, and you'd yip for her like a trained poodle."

"Damn straight," I grumble, flushing to the tips of my frozen ears. I shove my fists into the pockets of my leather jacket, hunching against their teasing.

"Look, you Nosy Nellies can get back to whatever it is y'all were up to, yeah? I got a groveling campaign to get to. First, where is Faye?"

The guys close in around me, meaty hands landing on my shoulders in solidarity.

Even Coach gets in on the action, giving my neck a fatherly squeeze. "She's already in the competition section."

Squaring up, I scan the crowd for Red's tell-tale tresses.

"LADIES AND GENTLEMEN!

A nasally voice booms from the central stage, distracting me from my freckled prey. "Welcome, one and all, to the Seventy-Fifth Annual Snowfield Springs Baking Competition, brought to you by the mayor's office!"

A smattering of polite applause ripples through the audience as a weaselly-looking dude in oversized dungaree screams into the mic.

"I'm your host, Phineas Pucker, and we've got an exciting lineup of local talent for you today! If you can bake it, you should be able to eat it!"

I tune out the grating jabber, still scouring the square for my favorite redhead.

There! A telltale flash of red near the stage stairs, petite and vivid.

My heart takes a giddy hop in my chest as I drink her in.

Fuck, I've missed her.

Missed everything about her. The way her nose scrunches when she's flustered. The constellations of freckles dusting her dimpled cheeks. That cherry mouth always quirking with some sassy quip...

I'm moving before I realize it, the compulsion to get to her, hold her, beg her, nearly suffocating.

But just as I'm muscling through a knot of chattering grannies, Weasel-Face trills into the mic again.

"Here to dazzle us with her Lemon Lavender Dream Pie, a celebration of spring's return, please welcome Baker Number Three, MISS FAYE WILLLLLIAMS!"

The roar that goes up nearly topples me off my boots.

Hoots and hollers bounce off the storefronts as my Red takes the stage, smiling shyly.

I'm stunned immobile as she waves to the clamoring spectators, her blue eyes sparkling.

Cupping my hands around my mouth, I suck in a lungful of pine-scented air and bellow, "FAYE! FAYE WILLIAMS! YOU CAN DO IT, RED! KNOCK THEIR SOCKS OFF!"

There's silence.

Dead, pin-drop, open-mouthed silence.

A hundred shocked stares swing my way, but I only have eyes for the absolute angel on stage.

Her eyes widen to the size of hubcaps.

Gut clenching, I flash her my best innocent grin, miming a 'let-me-be-your-cheerleader' shrug.

The heat of a hundred speculative gazes prickles my skin, but I refuse to look away.

I've made some damn questionable choices, I know that. But letting this gorgeous, genuinely good woman think for one second that I don't worship the air she sneezes is the biggest mistake of my life.

And I'm sure as shit not above making a public spectacle of myself to convince her.

I should have called. I should have groveled.

After a prolonged, breathless beat, the crowd explodes into fresh titters and cheers.

"WOO-HOO, FAYE!"

"SHOW 'EM HOW IT'S DONE, HONEY!"

"MAKE OUR TOWN PROUD, SUGAR—OH MY GOD, PATRICE, IS THAT TRISTAN BANE?!"

Faye gapes at me for a moment longer. But slowly, shakily, she raises the hand not desperately clutching her pie pan...and wiggles her fingers at me.

Sweet puck, I've missed that coy little finger-wave.

"Ahem," Weasel-Face coughs into the mic, brows arched damn near to his weird little fedora. "If we could get back to the contest? Miss Williams, your pie, please?"

Falling into an awkward half-curtsy, Faye shuffles forward, her braided curls swinging like a pendulum against her flushed neck.

Gingerly, she places her pie pan on the judges' table, shooting them a timid grin.

My lungs seize at the sight of her, all prim and rosy-cheeked in her candy-striped apron.

It takes every ounce of willpower I possess not to vault onto that stage and kiss her stupid in front of God and Snowfield Springs.

So I watch, heart in my throat, as she retakes her place in line, spine stiff with nervous tension.

The judges cut into her burnished crust and pristine meringue, forking fluffy bites into their smacking mouths.

An eternity of tasting later—or maybe just a few torturous minutes—Phineas Pucker snatches up an embossed envelope, his beady eyes shining with smug satisfaction.

"Well, folks, the results are in! It was a tough decision, as all our talented bakers brought their A-game. But there can only be *one* Supreme Baking Queen of Snowfield Springs!"

My hands clench at my sides, nerves strung tighter than old man Gunnar's banjo.

Stop milking the drama and give her something to celebrate...

"And your winner, of the Seventy-Fifth Annual Snowfield Springs Baking Competition is..."

Pucker pauses for what he clearly thinks is dramatic effect. I fantasize about cramming one of Diesel's rancid skate guards down his smug gullet.

"MISS FAYE WILLIAMS AND HER LEMON LAVENDER DREAM PIE!"

Chaos. Pure, unmitigated chaos.

The crowd surges forward, a tidal wave of flailing limbs and ecstatic hollers.

I'm carried along with the crush, dizzy elation filling my chest.

Somehow, I find myself tumbling onto the stage, hands stretched out.

Faye's face fills my vision, tear-streaked and glowing.

"I won," she croaks, almost disbelieving. A choked laugh hiccups out of her. "I actually won!"

"Of course you did, Red." My own voice is a gravelly wreck, thick with unshed emotion. "Never doubted you for a second. Come here."

And before God, Snowfield Springs, and the ghost of my mortified masculinity, I tug my jacket off to reveal a glaring purple tee.

Faye's name stretches across my chest in glittery capitals, right over my hammering heartbeat.

Her jaw drops, fresh tears welling in her eyes. "What...Tristan, what is that?"

I wink cheekily, fighting the urge to squirm under her gobsmacked scrutiny.

"I just thought it's high time I wore your jersey to show some support too. You deserve it."

"You know, Ben showed me the whole Julianna thing and your clarification post."

She swallows thickly, fingers tangling in her apron strings.

"Why didn't you call me?"

"Because there's no turning back now," I cut in fiercely, stepping closer. "I needed to brace myself...and give you space too."

Slowly, reverently, I cradle her dear face in my shaking hands, thumbs brushing her tears away.

My heart feels too big for my ribs, swollen with tenderness and the sweet, unfamiliar ache of love.

So much love I could choke on it.

"Most of my life has been a lie. My identity is mostly a lie. The perfect backstory for a golden boy."

My voice cracks, but I don't give a fuck. Not when her glorious eyes are glimmering at me like I hung the moon. "But you. Faye Williams, you've been real."

"Geez, Bane. You're making it sound like you have loads of imaginary friends."

There it is.

Her sass. Her wit.

"Something like that. Thank God we kissed on our first meeting." I shrug with a cocky smile. "It kind of sealed the deal. But now, no more lies or facades. Do you understand what I'm trying to say?"

For a breathless instant, she just stares at me, chest heaving with shallow bursts. I start to sweat under my collar, certain I've fucked it up somehow.

But then she launches herself at me, vibrant curls flying and her arms locking around my neck.

Her lips find mine with unerring accuracy, the sweet clash of tongues and panted breaths nearly sending me to my knees.

Distantly, I register the crowd's riotous catcalls, Slick and Diesel's wolf-whistles rising high among them.

But it's all just white noise against the symphony of Faye, the taste and touch and feel of my girl in my arms again.

"I love you," I murmur into her hair when we finally surface for air, my hands gripping her hips hard.

"So fucking much, Faye. I want to taste-test every new recipe you dream up and be your soft place to land at the end of the day."

I shake my head and look at her earnestly. "Sorry it took days to find courage for that short speech. But what do you say?"

She's silent, tears streaming down her flaming cheeks. And then she's sobbing a laugh, nodding so hard I'm scared her head is going to fly off.

"Yes, you big dumb jock."

Her kiss tastes like cinnamon and benediction. "I love you, too, Tristan. Despite all the drama you bring into my life. Now, shut up and kiss me like you mean it."

Well, hell. That's the only play I wanna run for the rest of my life.

CHAPTER 13

FAYE

The faint scent of fresh flowers breaking through the thawing ice seeps through the cracked balcony door.

I sprawl across Tristan's obscenely large bed, the black silk sheets cool against my bare legs.

Propping my chin in my hands, I watch him putter around the room, collecting the leftovers of our whirlwind reconciliation—a sock here, a bra there.

Seems we got a bit...enthusiastic in our haste to reacquaint ourselves.

RIP, lace panties. You will be missed.

Almost two months of living together has taught me his morning routine.

The way he always starts on the left side of the room, how he folds everything precisely even when it's destined for the laundry.

"Enjoying the view, Red?"

Tristan's amused rumble snaps me out of my panty eulogy.

He stands at the foot of the bed, arms crossed over his deliciously broad chest, one dark brow arched.

The waistband of his low-slung sweats barely cling to his cut hip-bones, revealing a tantalizing slice of bronzed skin.

"Always." I flutter my lashes playfully, fighting the heat creeping up my neck. "A girl could get used to waking up to all...that." I wave a hand at his chiseled...everything.

Prowling closer, he crawls onto the bed, caging me underneath his big body. "Oh yeah?"

I hum in agreement, twining my arms around his neck.

"Yeah. In fact, I think we should make it a daily occurrence. You, me, this bed...clothing optional, of course."

Tristan grins wolfishly, nuzzling into my neck.

"I like the way your naughty mind works."

His clever fingers sneak under the black duvet, tracing maddening shapes on my hairless mound.

Desire, warm and languid, unfurls in my belly. But as much as I'd love a lazy morning tumble, we've got places to be.

Sighing, I wriggle away, smacking a consoling kiss to his pursed lips.

"Hold that thought, Bane. We've got a big day ahead of us." I roll off the bed, stretching my pleasantly achy limbs. "A day that requires clothing."

He grumbles but complies, scooping a shirt off the floor and tossing it to me.

I catch it with a grin, pulling it over my head. It falls to mid-thigh, the sleeves dangling past my fingertips.

Wearing your man's clothes is better than brownies. Just saying.

I start to hunt for my leggings, but a peek at Tristan's frozen expression stops me cold. "What? Do I have drool crusted to my face?"

Shaking himself, he swallows loudly. "No, I just...fuck, Red. There's just something about seeing you in my shirt..."

He trails off, clenching his fists like he's physically restraining himself from jumping me.

I smile a bit, buttoning the shirt with deliberately slow motions until my nipples are finally out of view. "Guess I'll have to steal your clothes more often, then."

A wicked light enters his eyes as they rake over me, lingering on the sliver of cleavage peeking through the gap.

"Sweetheart, what's mine is yours. Mi closet es su closet."

I snort a laugh, chucking a pillow at his smug face. "Settle down, Rico Suave. What are you doing on Saturday?"

Tristan groans, hauling himself up and over to me with a grunt.

He's sporting a wide grin as he palms my ass, pulling me flush against the hardened bulge in his pants.

"Just some physical therapy and some drinks with the boys after."

I wind my arms around his trim waist and stand on my tiptoes to smack a loud kiss to his scruffy chin. "Free up your evening."

"Sure…that's all I get?"

"Yup."

Grumbling about sassy, secretive redheads, he smacks my butt and trudges toward the bathroom.

Soon, the sound of the shower filters through the cracked door, followed by an off-key but enthusiastic rendition of "Whatta Man."

Snickering, I shimmy into my leggings and fix my wild curls into a topknot.

Tristan's still serenading the sprayer when I hear my phone ping from the nightstand.

Snatching it up, I grin at the message lighting up the cracked screen.

Cara-Bear:

> Yo, Cinnamon Stick! Are you dead?

> Should I send a search party?

> Did that man-mountain you call a boyfriend smother you with his pecs?

I shake my head fondly, thumbs flying over the keys.

> Breathing just fine, Care Bear.

> Will you be at the Springfest Sat?

Cara-Bear:

> No, I'm on rotation. Shucks!

> I wanna watch that hunk of yours try his luck at the pie eating contest. ;)

I stifle a chortle, casting a glance toward the bathroom. Somehow, I doubt pie of any kind is on Tristan's agenda.

★★★

"Surprise!"

Tristan's jaw goes slack as I lead him into the bustling town square on Saturday.

His stunned coal gaze darts from the delicate cherry blossoms dancing on the breeze, to the booths overflowing with spring delicacies.

"Uh, Red?" He leans down to hiss in my ear, his minty breath gusting over my cheek. "What the hell is all this?"

I beam at him, breathing in the warm, fresh spring air. "The Annual Snowfield Springs Springfest, of course! It's the best social event of the season!"

At his dubious look, I roll my eyes. "Come on, don't tell me a hometown hero like you has never experienced the magic of Springfest?"

His brow crinkles adorably. "Springfest?"

And I'm the stranger to this town?

"Oh, my sweet summer child." I pat his cheek, stifling a giggle. "You may be the king of the rink, but here in the square? You're a mere peasant."

"Is that so?" The beginnings of a smirk tug at his sinful mouth.

"Guess you'll have to show me the ropes then. Hopefully they'll be attached to your bra."

"You pervert!" I tug on our linked hands, pulling him into the fray.

We weave through the crowd of cheerful townsfolk, the air vibrant with laughter and the excited shrieks of children.

The warm, comforting aroma of lavender honey cakes and strawberry tarts tantalize my senses, creating a symphony of festive delights.

Tristan seems a bit overwhelmed at first, shrinking into his shoulders like a spooked turtle every time a giggling pack of kids races by.

But slowly, he starts to uncurl, his grin making more than one matronly citizen swoon.

Soon, the townsfolk descend upon him *en masse*, their faces alight with curiosity and naked adoration.

I watch with a fond grin as Mayor Abernathy pumps his hand, gushing about his slap shot.

Librarian Harriet pinches his cheeks, lamenting the length of his hair.

But it's the arrival of Bee that has Mr. Popularity squirming like a worm on a hook.

"Well, *hello* there, tall dark and delicious!" Bee teeters up on sparkly kitten heels, her neon scarf billowing like a sail. Her magenta nails latch onto Tristan's bicep with alarming tenacity. "Where have you been all my life, you muscly morsel?"

"I...uh..." Tristan shoots me a panicked look, mouthing "Help me!" I smother a cackle in my scarf, giving a jerky wave.

Fly, little bird. Test those glorious wings.

My amusement is short-lived, however, when Principal Meriwether jogs over, waving a frantic hand. "Miss Faye! Thank heavens you're here!"

His complexion is an alarming shade of red, sweat beading on his egg-smooth head. My brows shoot toward my hairline at his obvious distress.

"Principal M, hi! Is...is everything all right?"

He swipes a damp silk hanky over his face, swallowing convulsively.

"There's been a bit of a problem with the festival schedule, I'm afraid." His eyes dart to Tristan, who's currently suffering Bee's attempts at a 'sensual' massage. "We, um. We need an extra participant for the pie eating contest."

I blink, confused. "Oh. Okay. So..." I spread my hands, baffled. "What does this have to do with me?"

Principal Meriwether has the grace to look chagrined, wringing his hanky like a stressed housewife. "Well, I was hoping you could participate?"

Welp. Looks like I'm getting my pie-hole stuffed, and not in the fun way.

★★★

Principal M said nothing about the pie eating contest being hands-free!

My fellow competitors are an eclectic bunch. From chubby Farmer Jessup, gap-toothed Dennis, Timmy Rawlins, and Eunice Prickle, the town's resident eighty-something spitfire.

We sit at a long trestle table, bibs tied around our necks and arms behind our backs.

I eye my pie with trepidation, the ruby red filling glistening in the afternoon sun. *Baking pie is fun. Eating...not so much.*

"Contestants, take your marks!" Mayor Abernathy bellows into a bullhorn.

"Get set....GO!"

I fall upon my pie, sinking my teeth into large bites of spiced glop. The cloying sweetness coats my tongue, the buttery crust scratching my soft palate.

Around me, grunts of effort mingle with wet chewing.

Farmer Jessup appears to be losing steam, his ruddy face transitioning from crimson to pale at an alarming rate.

To my left, Eunice Prickle attacks her pie with single-minded intensity, her dentures clacking loudly.

These people are sure taking it seriously! Welp. When in Rome...

Steeling my jaw, I double down, inhaling pie filling like it's the antidote to a deadly poison.

My stomach gurgles ominously, the pressure in my gullet reaching critical mass, but I chug on.

"That's it, Red! Get in there, sweetheart!"

Tristan's shout rises above the noise, spurring me on like a jockey crop to the flank.

I chance a peek through my crust-clumped lashes to find him front and center in the crowd, fists pumping the air like an over-caffeinated hype man.

"FIVE! FOUR! THREE!"

The chanting of the crowd reaches a fever pitch.

With a burst of energy I didn't know I had, I cram the last hunk of pie between my lips just as the final buzzer sounds.

The resulting roar from the spectators nearly sends me off my seat.

"We have a WINNER! Faye Williams, everybody! Let's give her a hand!"

Thunderous applause rattles the paper plates as I'm hauled to my feet by a beaming Mayor Abernathy.

He unties me and raises my hand in victory. I wobble a curtsy, my free arm clutching my distended belly.

Sweet niblets. I feel like Violet Beauregard post-Wonka binge. Only I'm bright red. One more shimmy and it's pie-palooza all over the town square.

Before I can voice my distress, I'm swooped off my feet by a pair of brawny arms.

Tristan spins me in a dizzying circle, his chest vibrating with laughter beneath my cheek.

"Attagirl, Red! I knew you could do it!" He presses a smacking kiss to my pie-smeared mouth, heedless of the mess. "My very own pie-eating princess!"

The crowd looks pretty unfazed by our peck. They saw much more yesterday.

"Tristan," I groan, clutching feebly at his jaw. "Baby, I'm thrilled you're proud, but if you jostle me one more time, we're gonna have front-row seats to the Puke-O-Rama."

Shake before use definitely doesn't apply to girlfriends.

CHAPTER 14

TRISTAN

The hum of electric razors mixes with the low chatter of the team's teasing. The perfect background noise for my post-practice haircut.

I sink further into the worn vinyl chair, a hot towel draped over my face.

"Yo, Blade!" Doc's shrilly voice cuts through my relaxation. "The guys and I are hitting up Sully's for a cold one after Matty is done with his tattoo. You coming?"

I lift a corner of the towel and squint over at my stocky teammate.

He's slouched in the chair next to me, his shoulders straining the cape that's way too small for him.

"I can't, Doc." I let the towel drop back over my face. "I have to be fresh for the game tomorrow. Those Avalanches are no joke."

With the preliminary rounds behind us and the quarter-finals won by a landslide, we're heading into the semi-finals against the Andover Avalanches.

If we win this, we'll be in the championship series.

The guys around me groan in disappointment. Slick kicks the base of my chair, jolting me. "Come on, Blade! One beer won't kill you. Live a little!"

I'm pretty sure beer has killed someone before.

I sit up, letting the towel fall into my lap, and frown.

"Cool it, Lucas. I said no, and I mean it." I look around the room with my best "Dad glare."

"In fact, I don't want to see *any* of you guys at Sully's tonight. We need everyone at their best if we're going to make it to the Finals."

The guys grumble and go quiet, suddenly interested in their fingernails and the tile work.

Across the shop, Rufus, the old barber who's been cutting our team's hair for the last season, gives me a supportive wink.

"You tell them, Bane. These young bucks don't know how easy they've got it." He runs a comb through Diesel's brown buzzcut, clucking his tongue. "Back in my day, the coach would've had our hides if we even thought about a bar before a big game."

"Speaking of hides..." Slick turns toward Rufus, a mischievous glint in his eyes. He nods toward a skinny, shaggy-haired kid bent over Matty's arm, a tattoo gun buzzing.

Rufus's face breaks into a proud smile. "That's my grandson, Levi. The kid's got real talent for tattoos, if I do say so myself."

We all lean in to check out the tattoo artist at work. Levi glances up, his cheeks turning red as we stare.

In the bright shop lights, he looks like a baby, barely able to grow facial hair.

Slick whistles, eyebrows shooting up. "Damn, Gramps. How old is he, twelve? What is this, 'Kindergarten Ink'?"

Rufus laughs and gives Slick a light smack upside the head.

"Watch your mouth, Martinez. The boy's nineteen. Just finished his apprenticeship last month. Wait...a bunch of tough guys like you would be the perfect test subjects for him. What do you say, boys? Want some Levi originals?"

The guys cheer and rush to be first in line. I stay back, grinning at the chaos.

These guys are wild. Show them a tattoo gun, and they lose their minds.

I spend the next couple of hours texting back and forth with my...girlfriend, eyes fixed on the naughty peek of her blue eyes underneath our chat pop-ups.

"Yo, Bane!" Matty's loud voice snaps me out of my thoughts. "Quit sulking over there and come check out Levi's work!"

Sighing, I get up and walk over to the crowd.

Matty shoves his arm in my face, grinning. "Look at this! Pretty sick, huh?"

I peer at the tattoo on his forearm. It's a super-realistic revolver with smoke spelling out **MAMA TRIED** in fancy letters.

Rufus wasn't kidding. Kid's got skills.

"Levi's an ARTIST, man!" Matty says, practically bouncing. "Who knew a little needle could make me look this cool?"

I roll my eyes and push his arm away before he takes out one of my eyes.

"Calm down. You're gonna pull something."
But I give Levi an approving nod, noticing his
pleased smile.

"Matty's right," Slick says, holding out his arm.
"Check this out. Isn't it awesome?"

I take a look at the lines of code tattooed in
binary on his arm and shoot him a bored look.
"Do I even wanna know what that is?"

"It's from the program that made me my first
million," Slick says proudly, rubbing his nails
on his Blizzard's jersey. "Back when I was just a
tech guy selling software to big shots in Silicon
Valley."

"Before Coach convinced you to use your skills
for good instead of evil, huh?" I joke, dodging
his halfhearted slap.

"What about you, Cap?" Doc sidles up with a
fresh skull and crossbones tattooed on his arm.
He nods at my blank skin. "Gonna let the kid
work his magic on you?"

I snort, crossing my arms. "No thanks, Doc. I'm
fine with being tattoo-free."

A smile sneaks onto my face as I think of red curls and freckles. "My girl already brings enough color to my life."

The guys groan and pretend to gag.

"Good *Lord*."

"I think I just threw up a little."

"Who are you, and what happened to the real Tristan Bane?"

"Let's just go." I flip them off with a laugh and turn to grab my stuff, but then Levi speaks up.

"Your girl...she's the pretty redhead, right?" Levi peeks at me under his messy brown bangs. "With those big blue eyes?"

I freeze. My throat feels tight. "Yeah." I pull out my phone and open my favorite picture of Faye, standing over a mixing bowl in just my team jersey. Of course, I zoom in on just her face. "This one."

Levi takes the phone, staring at her eyes in awe. "Wow. Those are like Disney princess eyes. Huge and bright."

The guys lean in, all trying to get a peek. Diesel lets out a long whistle. "Damn, never realized Faye has such gorgeous eyes."

"Totally," Matty adds, slack-jawed. "They're all...sparkly. Like, glittery or something."

"Straight up angel eyes," Slick chimes in with a violent nod. "But no one can compare to my Stella."

We all groan, unwilling to fall into another rant about his beautiful, amazing, charming, loving, caring, and wonderful girlfriend, Stella. *Geez.*

I slide my phone back into my pocket, feeling this strange, almost painful tug in my chest. A feeling I can't quite explain.

Man, I must be losing it.

Determined, I stride over to Levi's station, lying flat on his chair. The kid's eyes go wide, staring at me like he can't believe it.

"Uh, you sure, man? I thought you were, like, anti-tattoos or something."

I plant myself in the chair and look him straight in the eye. "I want my girl's eyes." I tap my neck. "Right here, over my pulse."

Levi's face lights up as he gets to work sketching her eyes out for me on a piece of paper. "One pair of angel eyes, coming right up!"

Ignoring my teammates' shocked faces and the grin on Rufus' face, I lean back and close my eyes.

A few minutes later, the buzz of the tattoo needle starts, and I let myself drift, imagining Faye's cinnamon curls, her freckles, and those sky-blue eyes.

★★★

The arena is packed to the brim with a huge sea of enemy colors.

Maroon and cream, the Andover Avalanche's signature colors, spread as far as I can see, with just a few small patches of blue and red for the Blizzards.

To be fair, making trips out for away games is pretty stressful.

The glass around the rink feels like it's vibrating from the crowd's roaring cheers, rattling through my bones like the bass at one of Diesel's crazy parties.

My hand tightens on my stick as I stop at center ice, the sharp sound of my skates swallowed by the frenzy.

I face off with Duchene, the Avalanche's enforcer, who's smirking at me from behind his cage, his mouth twisted in a sneer.

"Well, well, well." His annoying voice grates on my nerves, all friendly but full of venom. "If it isn't Snowfield's golden boy, here to run with the big dogs."

A muscle tenses in my jaw, my skin crawling with irritation. "Save it, Douche Canoe."

I give him a toothy grin, feeling a bit satisfied when he looks taken aback. "Talk smack, get whacked."

He glares, but before he can snap back, the puck drops.

It hits the ice with a loud crack, and we're off, sticks slashing and bodies slamming together as we fight for control.

I sink into the game's rhythm as the minutes count down to the end.

My focus narrows to the strain of my muscles, the cold air in my lungs, the pounding of blood in my ears.

This is where I belong—right here, where everything finally fits together.

My mates on the ice, my girl on the side.

Diesel and Slick on either side as we push up the slot. Time feels like it slows, my senses sharpening.

I see Duchene's attempt to check me coming from a mile away, a weak effort to knock the puck loose.

Nice try, jackass. But not today.

With a flick of my wrists, I slip a no-look pass to Diesel on my wing, grinning at Duchene's confused squawk.

Diesel nails it, the light flashing red behind the Avalanche goalie as he scores.

The muffled cheers of my teammates reach me as I leap into a chest bump with Diesel, his big glove smacking my helmet.

None of it compares to the sight of coppery-red hair that makes my heart race like crazy.

Faye.

She's leaning over the visitor's box, bundled in so many layers it's a wonder she can even bend.

Her cheeks are bright pink from the cold, and I can barely see her pointy chin over her huge Blizzard's scarf, but it's her eyes that catch me, sparkling at me across the rink.

Those eyes. God, I could get lost in those eyes.

Ignoring the whistles and jokes from my team, I pull off my left glove and hook a finger into my jersey collar, tugging it down to show the side of my neck.

There, standing out against my pale skin, is the result of hours of work from Levi.

A pair of eyes, big and bright, drawn in perfect detail. Her eyes, copied straight from my favorite secret photo, now inked on me for anyone with eyes to see.

I watch Faye's face as she realizes what she's seeing, her lips parting in a soft gasp.

One small hand rises to her chest, gripping her coat like it's the only thing holding her up.

For a second, we just stare, having a whole silent conversation with one shared look.

Surprise, Red. I did something big, something crazy. And I wouldn't take back a single second of it.

Her eyes shimmer behind those thick lashes, sending me a message only I can read.

Slowly, she nods, just a tiny dip of her chin that still feels loud in this huge arena.

Buzzing, I turn back to the face-off circle, my blood pumping like a shaken soda. Duchene's ugly face comes into focus, twisted in a scowl.

"Any time you're done making heart eyes at the puck bunny, Blade. Some of us are trying to win a game," Duchene muttered.

I ignore him, crouching into position. My stick presses against the ice, and I dig the edges of my skates in, feeling ready.

The puck comes my way, and I'm off like a shot, my skates slicing as I weave through the chaos of swinging sticks and crashing bodies.

I can feel Faye's eyes on me, like she's marking me right between the shoulder blades.

I've got a last chance to make happen with this championship, one final win for m—

WHAM!

A wall of maroon slams into my side, knocking me head over heels across the ice.

I hit the ice hard, my helmet smacking against the boards with a sharp crack. For a moment, everything goes blurry, the sounds fading.

I faintly hear a high, piercing scream, raw and awful.

Huh. Is that Faye? She sounds…scared. Why's my girl scared? Gotta…tell her I'm okay. I just need a minute to rest…

I try to move, to roll onto my back, but nothing's cooperating.

My whole right side is screaming, the dull ache in my knee suddenly exploding into white-hot pain.

And then, between one blink and the next, everything…fades.

It's like someone's slowly turning down the volume on reality until all that's left is soft, comforting silence.

CHAPTER 15

FAYE

The buzzer rings, signaling the end of the game.

Confusion is palpable in the announcer's voice as he announces, "The Snowfield Blizzards win. They'll be major contenders in the finals!"

Icy dread clogs my throat as I scramble down the stands, my legs numb beneath me.

The arena is filled with shocked gasps and rustling nylon, but it's all just white noise against the roaring in my ears.

Tristan! Oh God, Tristan!

He lays crumpled against the boards like a broken doll, his limbs splayed at unnatural angles.

"Tris? Baby?" I croak as I reach him, my voice a reedy thread.

Sinking to my knees, I reach out to his helmeted head, unsure of how to touch this suddenly fragile man.

Please. Please wake up. Snark at me, smirk at me, do ANYTHING...

A siren's wail cleaves the air, the clatter of a gurney. Paramedics in neon parkas swarm us, their chatter indistinct beneath the blood roaring in my ears.

I cling to Tristan as they load him up.

"Best let our girl ride with him, boys," Coach says quietly. "Seeing as how she's all the family he's got right now."

Hot tears spill down my cheeks at his graveled words, a hitching sob lodged in my throat.

I'm not family. Not really. But right now, I feel like the only thing holding him together.

For one blessed instant, I'm back in that kitchen, watching sunbeams play over the peaceful curves of Tristan's face.

I'm branding each scar, each blemish to memory.

"Faye!" Slick's urgent shout cuts through my grief-soaked haze. He jogs alongside the gurney, his dark eyes stark behind his helmet. "Let me go."

"Ignore him." Coach meets my gaze squarely, a muscle ticking in his jaw. "You go first. We'll clean up and join you later."

I sag bonelessly against the gurney, relief and gratitude washing over me. *Thank you.* I mouth, pouring every ounce of sincerity into the inadequate words.

Thank you for loving him.

"Family only," the lead EMT speaks dispassionately, already moving to shut the double doors.

I scramble up into the bay before I lose my nerve, wedging myself onto a tiny slice of bench.

Tristan's head lolls inches from my knee, and I thread a trembling hand through his hair, my palm molding to the beloved shape of his skull.

Please. I mutter a prayer out into the nothingness, my soul flayed and writhing. *Please, let him be okay. I'll do anything.*

★★★

"...surgery. As soon as possible."

My eyes feel like sand as I blink, Dr. Emi's brisk tone filtering through the static in my head.

She stands over Tristan's bed, her delicate features pulled tight with concern.

Beside her, Coach looms like a stone statue, his broad shoulders slumped under an invisible weight.

"He's...it's THAT bad?" I cry, my voice rusty.

It feels like years have passed since they wheeled him in. But I know it's only been a few hours.

Tristan never talked about the extent of his injury...and I never really asked. I was so stuck in my romantic daydreams that I never cared enough.

Dr. Emi's almond eyes soften, empathy radiating from her in waves. "I'm afraid so, Faye. That tumble exacerbated his situation."

She gestures to an array of X-rays clipped to a light board, blue-white images that makes bile surge in my gullet.

"See this? And this? His tendons are taking the heat. If we don't get in there and clean up the mess..." She presses her lips into a bloodless line, her meaning clear.

But Tristan doesn't want it.

"No." I'm on my feet before I realize I've moved, quaking all over. "No, he's...there's gotta be something. Rehab or exercise or—"

"Red. Breathe."

Coach's hand on my shoulder is an anchor, tethering me to reality. I shrug him off, whirling to pin Dr. Emi with a desperate stare.

"What about rehab? He's been making progress, I know he has!"

Dr. Emi sighs. "Progress, yes. But now it's all ruined, this just amped up from a grade one tear to a two bordering on three." She levels me with a look, kind but resolute. "This is his life we're talking about, Faye. His ability to *walk*."

"But...but the game." It bursts out of me, high and thready with panic. "The...the championship…"

Coach's sigh is a forceful wind, gusty and pained. "No game is worth a man's leg, girl. Not even the big one. Tristan might be okay until then, but one slip and his career could be over."

I want to scream, to rail at the injustice of it all, but the fight seeps out of me like water from a cracked pitcher, leaving me hollow.

Slowly, I sink back into the chair at Tristan's bedside, snagging his limp fingers in mine.

Dr. Emi turns to Coach, her slim fingers holding out the clipboard. "As his legal guardian for medical decisions while with the team, we need your signature to proceed with the surgery."

So fast?

I leap up, snatching the clipboard before Coach can take it. "Wait!" My voice cracks. "Please...just wait."

Coach's expression softens with understanding.

"Faye, sometimes we have to make the tough calls. That's what being a guardian means."

"But he trusted you with that power for hockey decisions, not..."

I swallow hard, staring down at the dense lines of printed legalese in Coach Bates hands.

This holds my whole world in its sterile grasp—the future of the man I love, reduced to a scribble of ink.

"He...he's gonna fight this," I whisper, tracing one fingertip over the signature line. "Hockey is his life. The only thing that...that makes sense to him."

The only thing he has left.

"That's why we need you to talk to him, Red." Coach gives my shoulder a bolstering squeeze, ducking to catch my gaze.

"Our boy? He's a stubborn one. Got it in that fool head of his that he's only worth a damn on the ice." His face pinches, exhausted and sad. "You know different, though. You see the man behind the mask."

Hot tears well up, blurring the document.

Coach is right. In our stolen snatches of intimacy, our conversations tangled in sheets and secrets...

I've glimpsed the lost little boy Tristan tries so hard to bury. The one who truly believes his only worth lies in his ability to play.

If he only knew that his smile, slow and real in the weak morning sun, is what sets my pulse racing.

That his quick wit and brutal honesty, given so carefully, so sparingly, is what keeps me orbiting him like my own personal sun.

You're so much more than your stats and your scars, Tristan Bane. And it's high time someone showed you that.

Coach looms in my periphery, his big knuckled hands flexing on his hips.

"Look, Faye. I won't...I won't lie to ya. This isn't gonna be easy. That boy's gonna buck like a bronco as soon as he gets wind of a scalpel," Coach says.

Dr. Emi makes a soft sound, her eyes brimming with sympathy.

"Coach is right, hon. Tristan...he's not going to understand. Not at first. But this? It's what's best. For his health, his future. It's what someone who loves him would choose."

Blinking against the hot sting of tears, I stare down at our entwined hands on the side of his bed.

He's knocked out on pain meds.

An image flits through my head, there and gone: those same hands, wrinkled with age but no less strong, reaching for me across a sun-dappled porch.

A squealing grandbaby on one knee and a slobbery bulldog on the other.

Peace. Rightness. Home.

I nod. "Okay, Coach. I understand."

CHAPTER 16

TRISTAN

The first thing I notice is the smell. That unmistakable, antiseptic stench that can only mean one thing: hospital.

It fills my nostrils, sharp and cloying, dragging me up from the depths of unconsciousness like a fish on a hook.

Beep. Beep. Beep.

The second thing I notice is the noise. A steady, rhythmic beeping that seems to drill directly into my skull, chasing away the lingering shadows.

Where...where am I? What happened?

I try to open my eyes, but they feel weighted, glued shut by some invisible force. Panic starts to bubble up in my chest, thick and cloying.

I can't move, can't see, can't—

"His surgery will just…Tristan? Baby, can you hear me?"

Faye.

Her voice cuts through the fog like a beacon, drawing me back to myself. I latch onto it, let it pull me forward into the light.

With a herculean effort, I crack open one eye, then the other.

The world swims into focus, a blur of white walls and sterile surfaces. And there, haloed in fluorescent light like some kind of fiery angel, is Faye.

She's a mess, her riot of red curls tangled atop her head and her normally clear skin is puffy and pale. But her eyes…god, her eyes.

They're like a shot of pure adrenaline to my sluggish heart.

"Red?" I croak, my voice a rusted-out husk. "What...what are you doing here?"

She lets out a watery laugh, her fingers tightening around mine. *Huh. When did she start holding my hand?*

"Where else would I be, you big dope?" She sniffles, swiping at her damp cheeks with her free hand. "You really know how to scare a girl, Bane. Thought you were gonna sleep for a hundred years."

I frown, trying to piece together the fractured shards of my memory.

I remember the game, the roar of the crowd, the adrenaline singing through my veins.

I remember Duchene's ugly mug, twisted in a sneer as he barreled towards me.

I remember the sickening crunch of impact, the explosion of pain in my knee—

My knee.

Ice floods my veins, my heartbeat kicking into overdrive. I jerk upright, ignoring the screaming protest of my battered body.

My gaze drops to my leg, swaddled in bandages and propped up on a mountain of pillows.

"No," I rasp, horror clawing at my throat. "No, no, no. Tell me they didn't...Faye, tell me you didn't let them—"

"Tristan, I—"

"I'll miss the finals," I whisper, my voice coming out hoarse. "The championship. Fuck, Faye, I can't—"

I break off, a sob tearing out of me like barbed wire.

This can't be happening. It can't.

What if the surgery doesn't help? What if all the time off for recovery totally destroys my form and game-play?

All I need is one more fucking win!

Hockey is the only thing that makes sense in this stupid, messed up world. Without it, I'm...I'm nothing.

"You let them cut me open?" I choke out, betrayal a barbed wire fist around my heart. "You let them...Faye, how could you?"

She flinches like I've struck her, fresh tears spilling over her freckled cheeks. "Calm down, Tristan. I didn't!"

"She's right, son."

Coach's gravel-rough voice cuts through my panic, yanking my gaze to the doorway. He's standing there, broad shoulders slumped, his face haggard.

"Take a goddamn breath."

"How can you tell me to—"

"I DIDN'T LET IT HAPPEN, YOU JACKASS!"

Faye's shout rings through the room like a gunshot, shocking me into silence.

She glares at me, her blue eyes snapping, cheeks flushed an angry red.

"I didn't let Coach sign the fucking form, Tristan," she grits out, her voice shaking. "I couldn't. Because I know you. I know how much hockey means to you, how much you need it."

She takes a deep breath, swiping angrily at her tears.

"I know...I know that you'd never forgive me if I took that away from you. I hate you for putting me in this situation."

I gape at her, my brain struggling to process her words. *She...she didn't let him sign? But then—*

"Your knee's not totally screwed yet," Dr. Emi says dryly, stepping into the room. She's wearing green scrubs and a distinctly unimpressed expression. "But it will be, if you don't get your head out of your ass and listen to reason."

I blink at her, confused. "But...but I thought..."

"That we carved you up like a Christmas ham while you were out?" She snorts, crossing to the bed and yanking back the covers. "Please. What kind of hack do you take me for?"

Faye and Coach let out an awkward cough, looking away.

I glance down at my leg, swaddled in bandages and braces. Not the heavy plaster cast I was expecting, but still. It looks...bad. Really fucking bad.

Dr. Emi starts unwrapping the bandages with deft fingers, her mouth set in a grim line. "You're damn lucky, Bane. An inch to the left, and we'd be having a VERY different conversation right now."

I swallow hard, ice trickling down my spine. "How...how bad is it, Doc? Give it to me straight."

She sighs, peeling back the last layer of gauze. I glance down at my swollen knee.

The athletic tape had helped mask the worst of it during games, but even I can't deny it looks rough.

"Your ACL tear has worsened, combined with tendon bruising," she says bluntly, prodding at the joint with gentle fingers. I hiss through my teeth, stars exploding behind my eyes. "It's only going to get worse under any serious strain. I'd recommend surgery as soon as possible."

Faye chimes in anxiously. "How long is recovery time without surgery?"

"It's a gamble. He might get by for a few more games with bracing and ice, but the longer you wait, the worse the recovery will be if it tears completely."

The room spins around me, joy filling my soul. "So I'll be all good by the time finals come around next week."

Dr. Emi scowls, sharing a frustrated glance with Coach Bates. "Yeah...I guess."

Faye holds out one hand, her palm cupping around my jaw while her other fingers stay wrapped in my hand.

"This choice to get the surgery...it's gotta be yours, Tristan. I'll back your play, no matter what...until the championship."

Staring at this fierce, resplendent goddess who somehow deems me worthy, I turn my gobsmacked face into her palm, pressing a fervent kiss to her skin.

"You..." I croak, breaking down and rebuilding my strength in the space between breaths.

"You beautiful, crazy, woman. Thank you."

And then she's laughing through her tears, and I'm crying through my groans, our mouths clashing clumsily, noses bumping and teeth clicking, sweet and sloppy and real.

I pour every ounce of my devotion, my awe into that kiss, branding her.

Dr. Taylor clears her throat pointedly, but I just ignore her, my other hand fisting underneath the thick cotton of Faye's sweater. *Screw decorum. I've had a day.*

It's the bang of the door flying open that finally breaks us apart, a mix of heavy boots and jangling gear. My teammates.

I surface from the kiss dazed and drunk, licking the salt of Faye's tears from my lips.

The room erupts into a riot of questions, the guys all jockeying for space around my bed. But it's Slick's face I seek out, all ashen and haggard.

He meets my gaze dead-on, no bullshit, no pretense. A thousand words pass in that shared look, apology, understanding, and anger.

My eyes mist, my throat working hard to swallow.

"I...I'm sorry, guys," I rasp, realizing that I'm the center of a circle of bowed shoulders and clenched jaws. "I just couldn't tell any of you." I squeeze my eyes shut, the words bitter as bile.

"You dipshit," Slick snarls, a muscle jumping in his lean cheek.

His dark eyes blaze, something wounded and raw swimming in their whiskey depths.

"You think this is about weakness? About some bullshit, meat-headed pride?!"

He leans in, his forearm braced on my bed rail, until we're nose to nose.

The scent of sweat and freshly sprayed cologne envelops me, and I shudder with the force of it.

It's not my fault. Hockey is all I have. It's all I am.

Faye takes my hand again, lacing our fingers together. "You idiot, you're my boyfriend!"

Since when did I start talking out loud?

Must have been my fall.

Faye's eyes are shining with tears again, but there's a fierce light in them, too. A love so bright, it takes my breath away.

"She's right. This is about family, you colossal dumbass." Slick grits out, his fingers sliding roughly through his mop of sandy hair. "You're our brother. Not just on the ice, but in here."

He fists a hand over his heart, right above the Blizzards crest.

"Let us the fuck in, man." Diesel's bass rumbles, thick with emotion. "Stop trying to be every fucking thing, and just be our boy."

Laid bare, stripped of all my pretense under the loving scrutiny of the people who know me, I crumble.

My head drops forward, my shoulders hitching with great, heavy sobs.

"I'm sorry," I croak, snot and tears smearing into the collar of my hospital gown. "I'm so fucking sorry, boys. I never...I didn't..."

"Oh, shut up," Doc grumbles, batting away my blubbering.

And just like that, the tension breaks, my blockheads pile on me like a bunch of half-trained St. Bernards.

Slick bitches about getting my snot on his jersey, Doc giggles about his own indestructibility, Diesel just lifts the whole bed up by the frame and rattles it like a ticked-off toddler just to prove a point.

"What's the play, Bane?" Faye asks, her pink lips quirked up in a grin. "You sticking this out until the bitter end? Limping your way to glory?"

"Through hell or high water, baby. They're gonna have to drag me off that ice in pieces."

Coach Bates glares, fist clenching then loosening in resignation.

"You're as stubborn as they come, kid. But you know the risks. You tear it fully, and your career might be done."

"I know."

Believe me, I know.

"Then you better get to healing, Blade." Faye leans in to steal a quick, hard kiss, her tongue flirting with the seam of my lips. "I expect a championship cup for all my trauma."

Whooping, I crush her to my chest, burying my nose in her fragrant nape. "You got it, Red," I rumble into her ear, my palm molding reverently to the sweet curve of her hip.

I stare at her, her eyes brimming with love and concern.

At Coach, who's looking at me with so much pride, it makes my chest ache. At Slick and Doc, who are grinning like loons, ready to follow me into fucking battle if I asked.

And I realize...they're right. All of them. Hockey is my life, sure. But it's not my whole life. Not anymore.

Because I have Faye now. And the team. And a future that's so much bigger than just the next game, the next playoff series.

I have...everything.

"Also," I add, my raspy voice cracking. "I'll do it. I'll get the surgery…immediately after we win the championship. From the rink to the operating room."

Faye makes a sound that's halfway between a laugh and a sob, throwing her arms around my neck. I bury my face in her hair, breathing in the familiar scent of her—vanilla and cinnamon and home.

"I love you," I murmur into her ear, the words slipping out before I can stop them. "I love you so fucking much, Red."

She pulls back, her eyes wide and shining. "Tristan Bane," she whispers, cupping my face in her hands. "I love you, too. More than anything in this world."

And then she's kissing me, her lips soft and sweet against mine. I sink into the kiss, my heart so full, it feels like it might burst.

This, I think hazily, as whoops and catcalls erupt around us. *This is what it's all about. This is what makes everything worth it.*

CHAPTER 17

FAYE

The air in Riverdale Arena crackles with electricity, the crowd a seething mass of mixed colors.

The Falcons' home colors dominate every corner except our small pocket of loyal Blizzards fans in blue and red.

I perch on the edge of my seat, fingers knotted in the hem of my 'Blade's Red' jersey.

On the ice, the team captains square off for the puck drop, jaws ticking and eyes blazing in challenge.

At the face-off dot stands my own personal gladiator, his stance wide and shoulders taut beneath his pads.

Even from the stands, I can see the intensity radiating off Tristan in waves, his focus laser-locked on the puck.

The ref's whistle trills, and the arena holds its collective breath.

The puck plummets to the ice...and the battle is on.

The Blizzards blue and red clashes with the Falcon's green and gold in a dizzying kaleidoscope of color and motion.

Bodies collide with teeth-rattling thumps, skates carving divots and spraying ice. Sticks slash and poke, jockeying for control.

In the center of the storm, Tristan flies like a man possessed.

He's poetry in motion, all fluid grace and slashing edges. His skates chew up the distance between the lines, his stick an extension of his muscled arms.

He weaves through defenders like smoke, a monster in Blizzards' blue, leaving chaos and cursing in his wake.

Every inch the Blade, lethal and lovely.

Please, I think desperately, my heart a war drum in my chest.

Please let him be okay. Don't let him get hurt again. I can't...I won't survive it.

I don't realize I'm holding my breath until my lungs start to burn, spots swarming my vision. With a gasp, I force myself to inhale, the chilly recycled air searing my nostrils.

I've never been much for prayer, but in this moment, I'm willing to try anything.

Before everything changes. Before the surgery that could make or break his career, his spirit.

Before the long, grueling road of recovery that I know will test the mettle of his mind as much as his body.

As if he can hear my silent plea, Tristan's helmeted head swivels to mine, his visor flashing beneath the arena lights.

Slowly, deliberately, he raises his glove to his mouth and presses a kiss to the heart of his palm.

For me. Always for me.

Tears prickle the backs of my eyes, a sheen of salt blurring the sight of my boyfriend.

I mirror his gesture, pressing my lips to the slick polyester of his game jersey stretched over my thermal shirt.

The familiar scent of fabric softener mingles with the chill of the arena, grounding me in this moment we've shared several times now.

A tiny, secret smile quirks one side of Tristan's mouth, there and gone in a blink. And then he's off like a shot, powerful thighs pumping as he chases down the play.

My eyes zero in on his knee, taking in the slight bulge of the tape and bracing underneath.

But from that moment on, there's no stopping him. No containing him.

Slick feeds him a puck, and bang—top shelf, glove side.

Diesel parks his brawny frame in the blue paint, screening the opposing goaltender. BAM—five-hole, red light flashing.

By the second half, Diesel has the puck, and Tristan comes up from his rear.

With a shared nod between Diesel and Slick, the puck is passed over to Tristan with a smile.

God, they're so obvious with it.

The goalie drops into a wary crouch, stick sweeping in frantic arcs.

"SHOOOOOT! SHOOOOT! SHOOOOT!" the crowd screams as a joint primal plea to the hockey gods.

I dig my nails into my palms, my pulse pounding in my ears. *This is it. The moment of truth...*

Tristan's arm flexes, the puck leaping off the ice as if bewitched. It bullets over the sprawling goalie as he tries to block it, the red goal-light igniting like a solar flare.

Finally, the foghorn blares, raw and triumphant.

BOOM!

The arena quakes on its foundation as the crowd loses its collective mind.

The boys in blue mob the ice, gloves and sticks and helmets flying in a jubilant celebration. At the center of it all, beaming like a little boy on Christmas morning...

"TRISTAN!"

His name is a broken prayer as I scramble down the stairs, shoving through the crush of spectators. Tears stream unchecked down my cheeks, my smile so wide it aches.

"Tristan, baby, you did it!"

Strong hands catch me before I can tumble over the glass doors, hauling me into a crushing embrace.

The jolt of our bodies colliding knocks the wind from my lungs, but I couldn't care less, not when his hot, hungry mouth is crashing over mine, wild and ruthless.

I pour everything I am into that fierce, graceless kiss, my fingers knotting in his uniform.

He kisses me like a man possessed, like he wants to crawl inside my skin and live there, and I open for him eagerly.

Dimly, I register the explosion of flashbulbs, the rising tsunami of wolf-whistles and lewd catcalls from fans and commentators alike.

I'm sure we'll be splashed across every sports page tomorrow morning.

...but wrapped in Tristan's unbreakable embrace, I can't find it in me to give a single, solitary fuck.

Let them look. Let the whole damn world see how much this man is loved, cherished, adored...

"God, I love you." Tristan groans against my lips, his big hands bracketing my face, thumbs sweeping my tears away. "What did I ever do to deserve you?"

"Besides being the most stubborn man on the planet?" I hiccup a laugh, rising on tiptoe to feather kisses over his hot cheeks, his damp brow.

He laughs, butting his forehead to mine. "I'll show you stubborn, you mouthy little minx."

His lips find that sweet spot behind my ear, teeth tugging just right, and I shudder from my crown to my curling toes.

"Yo, Casanova!" Slick's booming heckle shatters the moment like a fist through a soap bubble. "Put Red down before you sprain her back! We got a Cup to drink outta, remember?"

Tristan grumbles into my neck, his damp lashes tickling my jaw. "Fucking killjoys."

Heaving a sigh, he pulls back just far enough to meet my dazed gaze.

He waggles his brows, a wicked smirk tugging at his kiss-swollen mouth. But before he can peel off any panty-soaking quips, the rest of the Blizzards pounce, a screaming mass of victory and brotherhood.

I'm passed from sweaty hug to sweatier pick-up, the fellas crowing their glee as they manhandle me like a favorite teddy bear.

Through it all, Tristan watches me with naked adoration, his face split in a gobsmacked smile.

And God help me...I've never felt so LOVED, so cherished, so utterly home.

★★★

The ride to the celebratory dinner passes in a blur of giddy chatter and wandering hands, Tristan's knuckles kneading maddening circles on my inner thigh.

By the time we pull up to the parking lot outside Sushi Genji, I'm a quivering mess, sticky with want and half-drunk with need.

But some of the bubbly joy fizzles and dies when I catch sight of Tristan's grim face as he shifts into park. His jaw is set, a muscle ticking in his stubbled cheek.

The fingers of his right hand flex on the steering wheel, as if itching to punch through something.

Uh-oh. I know that look. That's his angsty brooding face.

"Hey." I cover his hand with my own, stilling its restless clenching. He glances at me sidelong, something haunted and feral swimming in his onyx eyes. "Where'd you go just now? Is it the surgery?"

For a moment, he says nothing, his throat working around a swallow. Then, slowly, he drags my palm to his lips, laying a lingering kiss upon my veiny blue lifeline.

"I just..." He starts, his voice choked and chalky. "I hate this. Hate that after tomorrow, I won't...we can't..."

He breaks off with a frustrated snarl, his free hand slamming against the dash. "FUCK! Nine months, Red. I can't play for that long...thankfully, I can still fuck you. It's the only silver lining—"

He's sulking like a child!

"Is that why you're acting like it's the end of the world?" I frown, leaning across the center console to pull him close.

Always ready for action, he scoots his seat back, making room for me to straddle his thighs.

I smirk. "I could help you take your mind off of things."

Images from my raunchier romance movies flash through my mind.

Numerous positions of the woman taking charge, bringing the man over and to the brink of pleasure with the rocking of her hips.

I wriggle deeper into the circle of his arms, turning to press my cold nose into the steaming hollow of his throat.

"Mmm," I hum in agreement, drunk on his scent and the cinnamon-apple of his body wash.

My tongue flicks out to taste, and he sucks in a sharp breath.

"Game was great. Only thing missing now is the happy ending. The kind that ends in screaming and moaning and teeth marks on the skin."

A hard shiver sends me crashing back against the steering wheel as his hand delves past the waistband of my jeans, clever fingers gliding and stroking.

I gasp, rocking into his discovery of my aching pussy. A low groan rumbles in his chest at the molten slick he encounters.

"Fuck, Red. Always so fucking ready for me…"

Soon, wandering hands turn purposeful. His other palm smooths up my belly to cup my breast through my Blizzards jersey.

Thick, clever fingers pluck and roll my nipples until they pearl through the fabric of my sports bra and the jersey.

Each tug sends a bolt of need straight to my clenching core.

"Tristan…" I pant his name like a prayer and a curse, my nails digging into his flexing muscles.

My eyes lock on his. Blue against black. "We have to…fuck, your surgery's tomorrow, we can't…"

"We can. I need my good luck charm before they put me under, Red."

"I was…AH!…gonna give you Mr. Scuffington…" I protest weakly, even as I buck into his boldly exploring fingers, my soaked panties already pushed to the side.

"I appreciate the thought." He mutters into my gasping mouth, his thumb finding my clit with the practiced ease. "But I want something else. A little slick to tide me over till I can fuck you proper."

A broken whimper leaves me, my eyes rolling back in my skull. *Forget hockey, this man's true calling is pussy whispering, Fuck…*

He works me relentlessly, fingers delving and stroking, palm grinding, until my spine's a livewire, every nerve ending screaming for a climax.

Whimpering, I scrabble at his fly with desperate hands, need eclipsing reason.

He groans as I free him from his straining zipper, his cock hard and pulsing against my palm.

Somehow, we shed the bare minimum of clothing, the windows of the Rover fogging with our frantic breaths.

Then he's urging me astride him, the hot, tip of his erection notching into my dripping entrance.

"FUCK, Faye!" Tristan grates out as he hilts himself to the root, my wet heat clutching him like a vise. "Oh, fucking hell, you feel incredible…"

He sets a punishing pace, pistoning his hips so hard the car horn gives a stuttering blast behind me. But I can't slow down, I don't want to.

I'm way too drunk on his broken moans and the slap of flesh on flesh.

Time melts away, narrowing to the sweet drag of his body in mine, the rising pressure deep in my core.

His name is a prayer on my lips, an exaltation and a plea, my nails scratching his clothed back.

"Come on, Red." Tristan coaxes through clenched teeth, his thumb grinding mercilessly on my throbbing clit. "Drench me, let me feel you cu…"

With a high, keening wail, I detonate like a live grenade, my spine snapping taut.

Tristan swallows my cries with his hungry mouth, his own release boiling over seconds later, wet heat flooding my clenching depths.

Thank goodness for birth control.

KNOCK-KNOCK-KNOCK!

"Aw, fudge!" The curse leaves me in an agonized yelp, my ass thumping painfully on the round edge of the wheel.

Tristan snarls like a charging bear, disbelief and frustration warring on his ruggedly beautiful face.

Please don't be a cop, please don't be a cop. I will die if we get pinched for public indecency...

But when I lift my flaming face to peek through the windshield, it's not flashing red and blues that greet me.

Oh no.

It's worse.

Standing not three feet from the Rover, his weathered face doing a really convincing impersonation of a scandalized socialite...is Coach Bates.

Ohhhh shit.

EPILOGUE

TRISTAN

One Year Later

The rink is illuminated under the arena lights, the fresh sheet of ice gleaming like polished glass.

My boys are huddled at the center line, a riot of blue jerseys and flushed, excited faces. In the middle of everything is Faye's best friend, Cara, sticking out like a sore thumb.

"Alright, fellas." I blow out a deep breath, my pulse doing double-time beneath my ribs. "Backs straight, arms out. And for fuck's sake, Matty, PLEASE tell me you put on deodorant today. I don't need my girl passing out from your rank pits."

Matty flips me the bird, but sniffs his armpit when he thinks no one's looking. Slick cuffs him upside the head, his face scrunched in disgust. "Damn, stinky. I can smell you from here."

"Fuck off," Matty grumbles, elbowing him in the gut. "Like your own sweat is daisies and sunshine."

"CHILDREN!" Coach Bate's bark cracks like a whip, startling us all to attention. "I don't know about you, but I'd like to get this show on the road."

Chastened, we settle into formation. I blow out another breath. *This is it. The moment of truth. Don't pussy out now, Bane.*

"Uh, Bane?" Doc's thin voice cuts through my building panic. "You, uh...you GOT this, right? The thing?"

He makes a vague circular gesture at his left hand, fourth finger extended.

SHIT.

My stomach drops to my skates as I paw frantically at my pockets, my vision tunneling.

No. No no no, I can't have LOST it, not now, not when everything is riding on—

"Looking for this?" Matty waggles a small velvet box under my nose, shit-eating grin firmly in place.

I snatch it with a snarl, my palm slick against the plush surface.

"When...how did you...?" I sputter, glaring at his unrepentant smile.

He just shrugs. "I wondered how long it'd take you to notice your precious was gone, Romeo."

The rink erupts into groans and guffaws, head slaps and 'duuuude's raining down like artillery fire.

I scrub a hand down my face, giving serious thought to sending Matty for a quick twirl in the Zamboni.

But before I can exact any creative vengeance, Cara's sharp elbow jabs my ribs.

"Stow the macho posturing, Bane. Faye just texted that she's at the rink to deliver cupcakes to Coach," he says.

My head whips toward the stands, pulse thundering in my ears.

There, gliding down the steps like some kind of denim-clad fairy girl, is my very reason for breathing.

Faye.

She's got her unruly curls wrangled into a messy topknot, her cheeks flushed and freckled.

A dusting of flour clings to the front of her faded Kiss & Crumble tee, hinting at another early morning elbow-deep in batter.

In her hands is a tray of glistening red velvet cupcakes.

God DAMN. How did I get so fucking lucky?

As I track her progress across the stands, Cara leans in close, her breath gusting over my feverish cheek.

"Last chance to back out, stud. Are you sure you're ready to lock this down? No more wild oats to sow, figure skater asses to tap?" she says.

I don't even spare her a glance, my eyes glued to Faye's joyous face as she hops onto the ice, confusion crossing her face at the sight of Cara.

"I'm surer than I've ever been about anything, Cara." My fingers tighten on the ring box. "Your girl's it for me. The sun, moon, and stars. I'll spend every day proving it to her, if she'll let me."

Cara's hand lands on my shoulder, startling me from my Faye-induced fog. Her grin is soft, gooey as the center of a molten lava cake.

"Then go get your happy ending, Prince Charming. I'll be here to catch her when she swoons," Cara says.

Faye's Converse hits the ice with a teeth-jarring thwack, drawing every eye.

Her smile falters as she takes in the assembled motley crew, a furrow forming between her brows.

"What the…" She blinks, clutching the cupcake box to her chest like a shield. "The heck are you guys doing out here?"

Her eyes land on me and widen to the size of hubcaps.

In three quick strides she's on me, one bony finger poking accusingly at my sternum.

My heart lurches like a hooked fish, desperate to wrap her in my arms.

"Tristan James Bane, you'd better not be thinking about skating," she growls, her lush mouth pursed in dismay. "Dr. Taylor said light activity for another week. You wanna fuck-up that knee again, after all that rehab?"

I raise my hands in apology, fighting a grin. *Damn, I love it when she goes all spitfire on me.*

But as I open my mouth to defend my battered honor, a flash of white in my periphery snags my gaze.

I glance over Faye's fiery head...and nearly swallow my damn tongue.

My guys are lined up in a ragged row behind her, a line of puckish grins and flushed cheeks...and pristine white lettered jerseys, spelling out a message that looks like it was finger-painted by a drunk toddler.

Y M E R A M R

Oh, you mother FUCKERS!

Cara is the only one in the right position.

Faye's no dummy. She clocks my bug-eyed expression and spins to follow my gaze, the cupcakes wobbling precariously.

I watch understanding dawn, watch her features crumpling in shock.

"Marry me?" she reads aloud, her voice small and cracked.

"But...it's misspelled? And the Rs are...separated?"

For a breathless moment, no one moves.

Faye just stares at the linguistic massacre masquerading as a grand gesture, her bottom lip caught between her pearly teeth.

And then...she laughs.

Great, loud guffaws, the kind that originate in the belly and ripple out in waves.

The kind of ugly-crying, but so fucking relieved, that comes after an enter year of sticking with your boyfriend through weeks of recovery and physical therapy.

"Oh my God." She gasps, clapping a hand over her mouth. Tears stream down her cheeks, catching in her cute dimples. "You...you dorks."

The tension broken, my guys collapse into each other like a stack of Jenga blocks.

There's shoving and cussing and the unmistakable thwap of hands against heads, but through it all, Faye's eyes never leave mine.

They blaze up at me, blue as the ocean and glinting with mischief.

"So," she drawls, one brow cocked. "You going to get down on your good knee and make a married woman of me, or what?"

Bossy, sassy, and perfect.

Laughter rumbles in my chest as I wobble down to the ice, the cold seeping through my sweats.

I fumble the ring box open, the large diamond glinting in the rink lights.

"Faye Elizabeth Williams." I start, my heart kickboxing its way out of my chest. "Love of my life, light of my soul, royal pain in my ass. Will you—"

"YES!"

She barrels into me with all the grace of a giraffe, her strong arms banding around my neck. I rock back on my heels, catching her weight with a grunt.

"Yes, yes, yes, a thousand times yes."

I laugh into her hair, my eyes prickling suspiciously.

With trembling fingers, I slide the ring onto her fourth finger, marveling at the sight of her slender hand in mine.

My future, glittering up at me with all the promise of a thousand tomorrows.

Gotcha, Red.

Dimly, I'm aware of the whoops and hollers of my teammates, the smattering of applause from the cleaning crew in the stands.

But it's all just white noise against the thunder of Faye's heart pressed to mine, the salt of her tears on my tongue as I seal our pact with a searing kiss.

We're a mess—runny noses, blotchy faces, dopey grins stretching our cheeks.

The cupcakes lay forgotten at our feet, a flash of red velvet that Matty would be all too glad to devour.

My surgery went well, and I'll be back on the ice in a week.

Faye's bakery is doing amazing with two new branches here in Snowfield and another in Boston.

She's still living with me, although I'm looking into getting another house.

Something smaller and more cozy with a large kitchen.

I'll miss my pool, though, but I wouldn't trade this new beginning for anything in the world.

It's imperfect. It's glorious.

It's the start of our forever.

One knee, one ring...one shot at happiness.

"Best pucking kiss ever, Red." I mumble into the warm crook of her neck, my arms a vise around her waist.

Her laughter echoes in the arena, bright and true. The sweetest sound I've ever heard and will hear for the rest of my life.

Till the ice thaws and the final buzzer sounds.

THE END

If you liked this book, then you will LOVE to read **A Pucking Chance** by Julia Savan.

***

When Maya's scathing article derails Brett's hockey career, the last thing he expects is to fall for her. But when teaming up with her becomes his best shot at redemption, they soon end up living under the same roof, setting off undeniable sparks in this spicy enemies to lovers hockey romance.

***

Keep reading to see a sneak peek of this book!

A SNEAK PEEK

of A Pucking Chance

Falling for the enemy wasn't the plan. But when our worlds collide, I'm blindsided by our chemistry.

I should've known this feisty journalist was trouble.

Maya's scathing articles went viral—icing my hockey career and landing me on the bench.

Now she's swooping in, convinced that my comeback story is her golden ticket to success.
But it'll only work if we join forces.

This may be my one shot at getting back on the ice. But I know better than to trust Maya.

Yet every stolen glance pulls us closer. And each forbidden touch makes it harder to resist the game we're playing.

Soon, we're living under the same roof in a small town, chasing the redemption story of a lifetime.

My sister Isabella would kill me if she knew I was falling for her best friend.

But as secrets spill and the final buzzer sounds...

I'd risk it all for a pucking chance to make her mine.

Visit the Kindle Store to get your copy of A Pucking Chance

Or read Chapter One on the next page...

CHAPTER ONE

Maya

Spying isn't my usual tactic, but desperate times call for desperate measures.

My heart pounds as I press my back against the tiled wall of the locker room. I quietly adjust my ponytail and tuck myself into a dusty niche next to the back lockers.

My nose wrinkles at the sweaty and musty odor coming from the laundry bin next to me, which is full of hockey pads, gloves, and other gear.

Talk about rock bottom—hiding here just to get a scoop.

I shake my head in self-disgust but quickly shrink into the shadows as I hear the approach of post-game players, their sticks and skates clattering in the concrete hallway.

The Arctic Blades have just suffered their most crushing loss of the hockey season, and the air is thick with tension.

I strain to catch the team's heated exchange as they tramp into the main locker area.

"Why didn't you pass the puck, Brett?" a gruff voice booms, his voice echoing off the walls. "I was open and had a clear shot!"

Through a narrow gap in the second set of lockers, I see right winger Tim Watts clenching his jaw and glaring at another player.

"But no, YOU had to take the shot yourself. You lost us the game, Wilson!"

My eyes scan the locker room, and I suck in a breath as I see him. Brett Wilson. Star player and captain of the Arctic Blades.

I hate how my body reacts to him, but God, he is so freaking hot.

Brett turns around and angrily starts to tear off his game gear. "Don't put this all on me! We ALL screwed up out there!"

Brett's muscles flex as he grabs the hem of his compression shirt and pulls it over his head, his muscles glistening with sweat.

The sight of his broad shoulders and chiseled abs sends an unexpected jolt through me.

My eyes linger on the way his muscles flex as he tosses the shirt aside. His chest rises and falls with each heavy breath, as the intensity of the game and the argument course through his veins.

Curls of his dark, sweaty hair stick to the sides of his face, accentuating his piercing blue eyes.

It's then that I realize that my mouth is open, and I'm all but drooling. I haven't even jotted down a single line!

Come on, Maya, focus!

I grit my teeth.

This is my chance to get a good scoop on this story. As the only female sportswriter covering this Denver game, I can't waste this opportunity.

Besides, I'm not one of Brett's swoony fangirls who'll fall for him just because of his looks.

Working swiftly, I abandon the notebook, quietly sliding it into my shoulder bag.

I carefully open the voice memo app on my phone and start to record just as Tim unleashes another tirade at Brett.

"You're supposed to be our captain! What kind of a leader hogs the puck like that?"

Brett's face reddens, and I can see a perfect storm is about to erupt.

I eagerly lean forward, extending my phone triumphantly to allow it to pick up the impending explosion.

This is going to be good—Brett makes this too easy.

Suddenly, I lose my balance, and the locker door in front of me slams shut with a loud bang. Game equipment stored by the locker falls on top of me.

"Ouch!" I blurt out before I can stop myself.

The locker room goes deadly silent at the sound of an unmistakably female voice.

Darn it!

I frantically stuff my phone into my pocket and look up helplessly as Brett comes around the lockers. His teammates follow.

Brett's eyes widen in shock as he sees me, but he bends down to help me up.

Sheepishly, I dust myself off as my cheeks flush with embarrassment.

My mind races as he lifts my chin, searching my eyes for answers.

"What the hell are you doing here?" he demands. "Don't you know this is the men's locker room?"

Brett looks at me, confused.

Dressed in jeans and a small tee, I could pass for a fan.

But then he spots my press badge. His eyes narrow as he reads my name.

"Think it's funny, huh? Are you spying on me? Trying to destroy my reputation again, Maya Simpson?" Brett punctuates my name with contempt.

I square my shoulders and meet his glare with defiance.

"Your reputation is already bad. I'm just doing my job. Maybe if you handled your stick better, there wouldn't be anything to twist."

The room echoes with jeers from the team as the tension between us crackles like electricity.

Brett's teammates watch our exchange with a mix of amusement and curiosity, their earlier anger momentarily forgotten.

"You think you know everything, don't you?" Brett's voice is cold and cutting.

"Maya, you're just a gossip columnist with a press pass. Real sportswriters actually understand and write about the game."

Ouch.

That hurt more than all the equipment falling on me.

I cross my arms and muster the best professional expression I can after being caught kneeling on the locker room floor.

Brett continues, "Maybe if you spent more time focusing on hockey and less time trying to ruin careers, you'd actually be taken more seriously."

His arrow hits the target.

My face flushes with anger, and I furiously retort, "Maybe if you spent more time being a team player and less time being a jerk, you'd actually have a reputation worth defending."

He flinches involuntarily from my words before tightening his stance and towering over me.

"Get out," Brett says with finality, his voice low and dangerous. "Before I really lose my temper."

I don't need to be told twice. I turn sharply on my heel before storming out of the locker room.

Behind me, I hear the chuckles of Brett's teammates, but I don't look back.

I have a story to write, and this is just the beginning.

***

I storm through the door before reminding myself to tiptoe quietly to the guest room at the end of the hall.

I don't want to wake up my friend, Bella.

After all, she was nice enough to let me stay here with her in Cedar Falls while I covered the Denver game.

Brett Wilson.

I shake my head as I enter the bedroom, my cheeks still flushed from our meeting.

He's such an arrogant and stuck-up player. Sure, they made him captain, but his teamwork sucks.

I sit in front of my laptop and start typing away, my fingers flying furiously across the keyboard.

The room is dark, and the glow of the laptop screen illuminates the space around the desk.

Other than the sounds of me clacking away at the keys, the house is otherwise silent.

I pause as I read over what I've written so far. The headline reads: "Brett Wilson, Hockey's Bad Boy: The Worst Player to Ever Grace the Ice?"

My cheeks still burn from his accusations—and the sight of his toned abs. God, he was all muscle. And his eyes…

I shake my head. Jeez, I felt just like a giddy schoolgirl when I saw him.

Focus, Maya. You've got a job to do.

My eyes narrow as I remember how rudely he had spoken to me. He is everything I hate—a self-absorbed jock who only cares for himself.

Hotshot or not, he had the nerve to make all those accusations and treat me like I was some sort of spy.

Well, I mean, I *was* spying, but who could blame me?

Sports journalism is a male-dominated field, and it was always my dream to cover ice hockey.

My dad got me hooked when I was young, and after my parents tragically passed away in a car accident four years ago, it took everything I had to get that journalism degree.

After returning to my childhood home, I applied for jobs and took on multiple freelance writing projects to keep me busy.

But I was itching for my breakthrough as an ice hockey journalist.

I just didn't realize how hard it would be to actually make it.

My eyes feel heavy with fatigue and frustration as I type the conclusion to my article.

Sometimes, it feels like I chose the wrong career.

I've spent the past three nights writing reviews on last season's most-viewed games, and the lack of sleep is catching up to me.

I even managed to secure a ten-minute interview with one of the coaches, for which I had to pay a hundred dollars.

I wince at the memory. I had to *pay* them.

Even so, when I checked this morning, the engagements had been very low, and I was tempted to delete the stories.

The only thing that has kept me going for the past couple of years has been my best friend, Bella.

She was there for me in college when my parents passed away.

And even though it's been a while since we last got together, she was more than willing to let me stay here with her while I covered today's game.

She still believes I can be an amazing journalist, and that means a lot to me.

The last thing I want to do is give up and disappoint her.

I sigh.

I'm probably doing that already.

I initially had no plans of criticizing any player in my stories. Ever.

But I'm desperate, and I need a surefire way to get engagements going.

There nothing more enticing to angry sports fans than a story that mirrors their own frustrations.

With a deep breath, I continue typing, detailing Brett's lack of teamwork, the way his attitude is dragging the team down, and his personal flaws.

The words flow easily, each sentence a dagger aimed at his reputation.

I know this article is going to be devoured by fans eager to see him fall from grace.

My fingers tremble on the mouse as I hover over the "Publish" button.

I take a deep breath and pause, the room feeling colder as the weight of my decision presses down on my shoulders.

Is this really my only chance to make a name for myself in this cutthroat world of sports journalism?

I stare at the screen.

My ambition doesn't care about some hotshot's ego getting bruised, but my conscience definitely twists around at the thought of inciting another viral attack against someone.

Internet fans are always so eager to jump in and blow things out of proportion.

The cursor blinks, waiting for my next step.

I have to make a choice—follow my ambition or listen to my heart.

But didn't my heart tell me that Brett Wilson somehow was the key to my success?

He's an easy target, always rubbing somebody the wrong way with something he did or said on or off the ice.

"He deserves it," I whisper to myself.

With a sigh, I click "Publish" and nervously shake the jitters out of my hands.

The article is now live, and there's no turning back.

As I lean back in my chair, the glow of the screen now feels harsher and more unforgiving.

I've made my choice, but I can't shake off the uneasiness that I feel.

My career is on the line, but so is Brett's.

Just then, I hear several loud dings coming from my computer.

The first negative comments are starting to pour in.

I quickly shut my laptop and closed my eyes.

I don't want to think of the damage that I have just caused, even though Brett is the closest thing I have to a sworn enemy.

Visit the Kindle Store to read the rest of A Pucking Chance